Books by Ned O'Gorman

THE HARVESTERS' VASE

THE BUZZARD AND THE PEACOCK

ADAM BEFORE HIS MIRROR

THE NIGHT OF THE HAMMER

PROPHETIC VOICES

PROPHETIC VOICES

Ideas and Words on Revolution

Edited by
Ned O'Gorman

Random House New York

First Printing
9 8 7 6 5 4 3 2

Published in the United States by Random House, Inc., New York,
and simultaneously in Canada by Random House
of Canada Limited, Toronto.

Library of Congress Catalog Card Number: 67-22647

Manufactured in the United States of America
by The Haddon Craftsmen, Inc., Scranton, Pennsylvania
Designed by Andrew Roberts

CONTENTS

INTRODUCTION 3

PART ONE

Essays on Revolution 11

THE REVOLUTION OF PEACE by James W. Douglass 13

THE HUMAN REVOLUTION: A SEARCH FOR WHOLENESS by George W. Morgan 35

THE RACE REVOLUTION: REFLECTIONS ON A DYING REPUBLIC by William Strictland 58

INTERNATIONAL LAW IN A REVOLUTIONARY WORLD by Frans A. M. Alting von Geusau 68

EXCERPTS FROM A CORRESPONDENCE ON REVOLUTION AND LANGUAGE by Deirdre Levinson 105

PART TWO

Definitions in Revolution

TIME AND REVOLUTION by Freya Stark 115

Contents

SILENCE by Peter Minard 118

THE IMAGINATION by William Lynch 123

SYMBOL by David Rast 125

ETERNITY by Charles Hartshorne 130

ABSOLUTE by Charles Hartshorne 134

GOD by Charles Hartshorne 140

SHAPE? IMAGINATION? LIGHT? FORM? OBJECT? COLOR? WORLD? by Ad Reinhardt 149

World by John Nef 155

FRIENDSHIP by Vincent Harding 157

MARRIAGE by Michael Novak 160

PURITY by Thomas Merton 164

EUCHARIST by David Rast 173

World by Vincent Harding 181

NEGRO by Vincent Harding 183

CULTURE by Michael Novak 186

CULTURE AND CIVILIZATION by John Nef 188

POET by Dennis Gabor 190

LITERATURE by Michael Goldman 193

BEAUTY by William Lynch 196

JUSTICE by William Pfaff 199

LAW by Vincent Harding 200

SCIENCE by Matthew Lamb 202

World by William Pfaff 207

NATION by John Nef 209

Contents

PATRIOTISM by William Pfaff 211
FATHERLAND by John Nef 212
SOVEREIGNTY by Peter Steinfels 214
CAPITALISM by John Nef 216
MARXISM by Peter Steinfels 219
REVOLUTIONISTS by Hans Koningsberger 223
THE CROSS by Sister Mary Immaculate Creek, C.S.C. 227
DEATH by Thomas Merton 230
FREEDOM by Vincent Harding 239

PROPHETIC VOICES

INTRODUCTION

This book offers certain alternatives to destruction. For the militant, perhaps these essays are less than revolutionary. They were to have been about the strategy, the loci, the philosophy of revolution that pointed to the "overthrow," to the "downfall of cities and governments," to the "change" in history. But for reasons I shall try to explain, such a book was impossible. I was incapable at the beginning of this task to make judgments about myself; they had to do with my sense of fatherland and my country's notions about power.

In 1965 I was sent off by the State Department to Chile, Argentina and Brazil as a cultural representative of the United States. (A "cultural representative" did not sound as vulgar and absurd then as it does now.) In 1965 I thought an intellectual had more to do with ideas than bread. I arrived armed with ideas. All of them I reckoned revolutionary, "liberal," and sure to get across the notion that America was in trouble indeed but she was a land, too, of revolutionary hope. I spoke with gusto and delight about poetry, religion, race and education. I thought my credentials impeccable. I wrote poetry. I had taught in the South. I had been an editor at *Jubilee* magazine, at one time a lucid, and in a small radiant way, progressive Catholic journal; I'd come up against the law in the university and the government. I was, I thought, no mere babbling poet, rummaging in his bag of memories for wit and song. But in South America I discovered I had no idea of politics; I had been isolated in the world of my poetry. I saw everything through the joyful forms of the imagination and my regal and golden childhood. But my hope was untried, my patriotism swathed in that optimism that corrupts all our politics and in a naïve cheerfulness that believed in the good intentions of my government.

(I ought to have suspected something was wrong when the embassy in Buenos Aires sent home a report, after the first week of my visit to Argentina, that not since the Harlem Globe Trotters had there been such a visitor as myself to South America. I did not distrust then, as I do now, the "enthusiasm" of the diplomatic corps.)

In May 1965 I was jolted from poetic fancy into the real world by a revolution. I was visiting Córdoba in northern Argentina when history, broken and suffering, touched me: America had landed marines in Santo Domingo. "Yankee, Yankee, *asesino,*" shouted wandering mobs of angry Argentines; the American embassy was stoned. I asked the men attached to me from the embassy to tell me what had happened. (Santo Domingo was a meaningless word to me; I knew nothing of South American revolutions or governments except for those liberal slogans I had gathered from some types I knew on the "left.") America suddenly seemed to be hated by everyone I met. I thought we must be right—hasty, a bit too frightened, but ultimately right. And I was assured by the embassy in Argentina that all was well. "Be a poet," they said. "When you are asked about the invasion, say that you are a poet and ought not to be expected to know about such things. Say you are not prepared." But I insisted on being told the facts and they told me. They had no reason to think that I would not follow the State Department's interpretation of those facts. They all told me—ambassadors and secretaries, consuls and cultural affairs officers—that the invasion was a disaster but they had no choice but to defend it. I had no choice, they said, since I was in the employ of the State Department, but to defend it, too. The more I was assured that all was well, just and necessary (the facts notwithstanding), the more I knew that the United States had blundered with moral violence and brutality into a revolution it could not tolerate or understand, so blinded were Americans and the State Department by a terror of communism. When I declined assent to Embassy orders to follow State's policy they raged—one officer wept, one called me a traitor, another threw road blocks in the way of my travels in Brazil by canceling lectures, flying me over enormous distances at a moment's notice and letting me while away hours beside swimming pools waiting for contacts that never came. Only when I took up mild intellectual arms against my countrymen did I make fleeting contact with the visionaries the embassies feared, avoided and tried to keep from me. As the days passed by, anger and despair grew: I looked into the face of my country—a frightened, brutal, counterrevolutionary face.

I had to become a poet and a citizen. I talked to everyone I met about democracy, about revolution, about man, freedom, the black man and the Church. No one at our embassies in Chile, Argentina and Brazil cared to talk about democracy, freedom, self-determination, the United Nations, the Association of American States, truth, history —all such ideas were reduced to the uses of "policy." Democracy to our diplomatic corps was a bad memory to be defended, praised or blamed in the light of a foreign policy wracked with fears of Che Guevara, communism and rioting peasants.

This book, then, is the effort of a poet without a homeland (for I have lost the sense of patria; I learned again to love America through the black people and their revolution—but that is another story) to discover the revolutionary who sees that what was has to go or men will perish, and to search for the prophetic visionary who knows what must be done so that men may endure in peace and joy.

When I wrote to Cuba, South America, Africa, China and India and asked men there to write of their vision of revolution, I had no idea that when they learned in my letter I had just returned from a trip to South America sponsored by the State Department they would think me, not a poet on an innocent expedition, but a spy, patsy, dupe of the State Department, the FBI, the CIA, which were notorious all over the world for baroque political amorality, bearing gifts of counterrevolution and war to the poor and hungry.

So, misunderstanding my motives, the activists who were readying the world for change, peaceful or violent, cut themselves off from me. The men who did write wrote out of their hope and vision of man. On the verge of destruction man is unable to feed the poor, stop the arms race, war, racial slaughter and the deathly cycle of technology. This book is a meditation on work, law, peace, race and language—spontaneous, extravagant in hope, rich in wonder and history, and balanced with love and daring expectations. It hopes to point to ways of rescuing man from the terrible grandeur of wealth, speed, nationalism and the "winnable war."

It is dedicated to one woman, one group of women and four men who are acting out the expectations and alternatives described in this book: Dorothy Day, the revolutionary who loves the poor and builds a place for them in the midst of triumphant wealth; Daniel Berrigan, the prophet who loves the notion of peace so that he risks jail, mockery and loneliness to sing and speak of peace in the name of Christ and man; Bishop Helder Camera, the Brazilian who brings revolution and hope to the poor of the north of his land, risking the hatred of his fellow Catholics, the violence of the government and possibly death; Vincent Harding, the black man who seeks peace and revolution within the labyrinthine wilderness of the black man's beauty and torment; David Jones, the great poet, whose life, pure in its search for the word and serenely isolated in energy, is the parable of the vocation to poetry; and the Dominican Sisters on 129th Street—Veronica, Martha, Margaret, Justine, Jane—who seek out the wounded and heal. They work as every man who has written this book works—against the destruction that builds a citadel in the world. It is their energy, hope and joy that gave me the strength to finish editing this book.

Each essay is the result of a long gracious agony of letters, telegrams and telephone calls. It is not easy for a poet to convince serious minds and revolutionaries that it is worthwhile at all to get involved with a "poet's" conception of anything. Each man—the contributors to the dictionary and the essayists—wrote from the fullness of their spirit, hence the disparities of style, but hence, too, the unity of vision: man, his lamentations, his glory.

William Strickland wrote:

> Your description of the book is intriguing. At the same time it made me fearful. For when you speak of revolution as a "change in the fabric of existence" in the living of life itself, then you begin to scratch at some truths about America which have yet to be described. And the question, it seems to me, is, How do you get people to understand the workings of myth within their own country, within their own community, within their own family, within their own being?
>
> Many years ago I took a seminar with Dave Reisman. It was kind of a magic time in Cambridge. Erikson was there, Roger Hagan, Kenneth Keniston and many more. Everyone was bright and committed, and nearly all were poetic. We were intoxicated with ourselves. And one day, it became clear to me that everything was not real—that our imaginations and sensibilities had betrayed us. Because we were wishing so very, very hard. But wishing would not make it so.
>
> If your book is to be relevant to the world, may not the fact of my responsibility and yours and Everyman's slip through? It seems to me that all things begin with human life. In that way, I feel the very strongest ties exist among the revolutions you divide into four. They are all related.
>
> What I also miss in your draft is the terror and the horror and the madness of men. One cannot talk about man's virtues without in some way talking about his crimes, for these, too, are related. Life and death, good and evil, black and white, rich and poor, these are the dialectics of our time. Things do not just happen. If it is

true, as I believe, that we are nearing a prerevolutionary situation in America, how are we to make known the truth when it is precisely the truth that drives us mad?

What I want you to do, I guess, is to take a stand, to dig into the substructure of rationalizations, the dung of myth, and say, This is right, this is wrong.

A word about the dictionary. When I struggle with a poem, I know how language is strangled in this age by fear, war, television, class idols and a cosmic kind of vulgarity. The dictionary brings certain words back to life to rescue them from death on the thoroughfares. I sought lively definers who loved language, treasured words and had an easy and happy way with problems of definition. The dictionary fills in the spaces between the essays, within the essays. It brings the book into the cosmos of art, eternity, color, fatherland, imagination, beauty, marriage, purity, death, friendship.

N. O'G.

St. Catherine's Rectory
Riverside, Connecticut

ONE

Essays on Revolution

THE REVOLUTION OF PEACE

James W. Douglass

To see reality in our time is to see the world as crucifixion. Our age is defined by the kind of events, from Auschwitz to Vietnam, whose depth of evil imposes night on the eyes of countless victims at the same time that the executioners, removed yet responsible, hide behind blindness or comfort themselves with the self-righteousness of an ideology. To see reality is to cut through the blindness of self, whether that self be one of the individual alone or, more commonly, the extended self of family, race, or nation. To see reality is to cut through every self of our time so as to go out from the blindness of a few into the beauty and darkness of the world of man, given over to agony and despair by absent executioners. To see reality is to be wholly present at the crucifixion of the world; to live reality is to enter into that crucifixion, but to do so, in the phrase of Albert Camus, as neither victim nor executioner. The life of the living is a suffering with the world, yet not as a passive victim but suffering in resistance and in love, experiencing the darkness of crucifixion without surrendering the hope and strength and revolution of resurrection.

The event which revealed the essence of our age of global crucifixion took place in a city. It has been described more accurately by Shintaro Fukuhara, a boy then in the fourth grade, than by the distant objectivity of the movie camera recording the scene from within the B-29 bomber flying overhead. Shintaro was the B-29's target:

> The all-clear had just sounded after an alert and I was idly watching the increasing numbers of my friends who were arriving at school. A red dragonfly came swooping by and alighted on the top of the wall right before my eyes. I saw it clearly. When I think back on it I realize that even then I was hearing the characteristic sound of a B-29 engine, but lulled by the security and relief of the all-clear, I let the sound go in one ear and out the other. My little brother had just put out his hand to catch the red dragonfly on the wall when in that instant there was a flash and with my whole body I received a shock as if I had been thrown into a furnace. I was blasted into the angle of the wall. Even now when I think about it I wonder when and how it was that I, after being slammed around as one in a delirium from inside a swirl of light rays into instantaneous blackness, ever got hold of my little brother's hand and began to run. Only fragmentary glimpses of those scenes are left printed on my retina as on a photographic film.
>
> When I opened my eyes after being blown at least eight yards, it was as dark as though I had come up against a black-painted fence. After that, as if thin paper was being peeled off one piece at a time, it gradually began to grow brighter. The first thing that my eyes lighted upon then was the flat stretch of land with

only dust clouds rising from it. Everything had crumbled away in that one moment, and changed into streets of rubble, street after street of ruins. I, who had unconsciously taken my little brother's hand and started to run, when I saw the cruelly burned passengers come rolling out one after another from a trolley-car, only ran the more wholeheartedly toward home, with fear for the safety of my family tightening itself around my chest.

The countless miserable things that happened at that time are quite beyond my pen and my tongue. Because of that calamity I lost my most beloved father and older sister. I will never be able to see my father and sister again forever. I know there are others who have lost equally—or rather, there are hundreds of thousands whose misery is many times greater than this, who have been deprived of everything that gave them happiness, and my feeling of indignation is only stirred up the more by the immensity of the disaster.[1]

Between the moment Shintaro's little brother reached out to catch the red dragonfly on the wall and the moment the two children began to run hand-in-hand through rubble and agony, man entered the age of his most critical self-revelation. He did not enter it accidentally or without warning. In terms of the sheer enormity of murder involved, even Hiroshima and Nagasaki were exceeded by the prior events of Auschwitz, Buchenwald, Dresden, and Tokyo. From a moral standpoint, the coming of Hiroshima was foreseeable in the paradox of the triumph and weary indifference with which Allied populations had responded to the reports of mounting atrocities by their own forces, which signaled their blind approval of the next step.

Hiroshima was no moral break from the pattern of obliteration bombing of German and Japanese cities. But it was a significant power break in the history of mankind, inasmuch as it revealed the power equal on a global scale to man's moral capacity for self-destruction and did so in such a way, in the agony of Shintaro and his city, that the new power instantly became one with the old drive to kill. Hiroshima was then the wedding place of final weapons—those through which mankind can commit a final act—with the death-instinct which prompted Cain to destroy his brother in the field. That new period, termed the Nuclear Age, has therefore become, in temporal and moral terms, eschatological; man is in confrontation with his spiritual depths. Hiroshima, where the Bomb and the Cain-instinct joined above Shintaro's playground, pressed on the human conscience the connection between millions killed in gas chambers and in burning cities and the power that is capable of ending history. There can be no escape in our age from the primary threat that man may commit the final murderous act.

The Nuclear Age has therefore brought man's quest for security through ever-greater destructive power to an absolute end. The historical pursuit of security through superior weapons has arrived instead at the insecurity of threatened extinction. For the first time in history, any further increase in man's destructive power is irrelevant to his situation in time. Whether the existing arms are capable of ending the human race once or a thousand times is irrelevant to the conscience of man, to whom a new revelation of the nature of power has been given. Military power has put all mankind on the cross.

But short of the actual use of apocalyptic weapons, mass murder is already the mark of our age. Nor is it confined to the atrocities of Algeria, Hungary, and Vietnam. Its global presence and nature can be defined statistically: "The amount of money spent on armaments today [by a few major powers] is equal to the total national income, not of any one country, but of the combined continents of Asia, Africa, and South and Central America."[2] While, according to the director general of the UN Food and Agriculture Organization, half of the world's population is "underfed or badly fed or both," the greatest industrial power in the world spends $30 billion a year to wage war in Vietnam.[3] The reverse side of the arms race and Vietnam is the sustenance gap in places like Palma di Montechiaro, a town typical of Sicily. When submitted to an inquiry into health and sanitary conditions, it was

> brought to light, among other facts, that tests for worms showed that "out of 267 children examined 74.9 per cent had threadworms, and out of 235 persons of all ages, mostly children, 34.5 per cent had dwarf tapeworms and 11.1 per cent had common round worms." That, naturally, "90.2 per cent of the houses are without running water and 86.4 per cent without lavatories. Only three of the eighty-two lavatories have a proper bowl and seat and only one of these is placed in a separate room." That, naturally, "the drains are practically non-existent and their place is taken by rivulets of black water which cut stinking furrows in the surface of the street." That out of 20,429 inhabitants, 4,964 are on assistance, most of these being under-employed. That "only one house, out of 600, was entirely free from mice and rats." And so on and so on. . . .[4]

The world of Vietnam and the world of Palma di Montechiaro are identical: they are the two arms of a single global cross. What is done by enormous resources of technology turned to destruction in the one is left undone by the lack of application of knowledge and technology in the other. The Vietnamese from war, and the desperate in Sicily, India and Latin America from indifference, are victims of the same process. As the economist J. D. Bernal has put it, "Now all scarcity—and this is really the most important thing—all scarcity, all need felt in the world, is henceforth due to human interference, human stupidity and human greed. The means are there, the knowledge is there; what is needed is the will to apply them."[5]

The power of the affluent not only threatens global destruction but actually carries it out in widening circles of famine and destitution. The jealous possession of such power renders man powerless to make peace, both because it commits him to the end of all peace on earth and because it already wages global war against the hungry.

To the man whose conscience is defined by his sense of humanity, the growing facts of such a world raise the moral imperatives of resistance and revolution. A political or economic system which can preach an ideological crusade against the poor punctuated by napalm and TNT or which can tolerate worms in children's stomachs, deserves uprooting, not allegiance. To the human family's threatened murder by nuclear weapons and to its continuing murder through privilege and indifference, the response of human conscience is No. In such a world, revolution is not a question and a possibility, but an obligation and a necessity. One must either revolt against the disorder of the present order or cease being human oneself.

Revolution begins in the revolutionary himself by his response to the present world, creating through the crisis of vision and shared agony the kind of power which rises to meet a torn world anew with the word of love and the act of transformation. The revolutionary has no other choice in love than to seek with his whole being a new heaven *and* a new earth.

But the revolutionary of the Nuclear Age, as the man

most sensitive to the realities of his time, must recognize that he, especially, lives under the cloud of man's ultimate powerlessness before military power. It is the revolutionary who, above all, must lead the search for a new power that can free man from the fatal illusion of power which apocalyptic weapons represent. The facts of power in the Nuclear Age have emphasized a truth of revolution as such, that to seek revolution through destruction is to commit the crime of denying the end by the means.

For to revolt against injustice is at the same time to revolt in favor of life, life in the world and life in oneself. As revolution passes from the thought of conscience to act, its true genesis must be in living forms, in means just as much as in ends. The death of the Russian Revolution carries a danger sign for all mass movements, since it lay in its subordination of actual life to a theory of life, of living men to principles and techniques concerning eventual happiness. When the revolutionary divorces ends and means and oppresses for the sake of liberation, he loses life and the source of his power. The new order absorbs the bitterness of the old, and the revolutionary-become-tyrant transfers his struggle against injustice to a struggle with the world as such, in all its forms and beauty.

But given revolution's inspiration, which was a cry of the living for the life they were created for, it cannot bridge the life and the living by means of a sword. It cannot fulfill life through death. It cannot create a new order of justice in murdering all those who had supported injustice—in this way injustice will merely have changed hands.

Pasternak's description of the revolutionary Strelnikov lays bare the temptation which, if accepted, marks the end of revolution:

> In order to do good to others he would have needed, besides the principles which filled his mind, an unprincipled heart—the kind of heart that knows of no general cases, but only of particular ones, and has the greatness of small actions.
>
> Filled with the loftiest aspirations from his childhood, he had looked upon the world as a vast arena where everyone competed for perfection, keeping scrupulously to the rules. When he found that it was not like that, it did not occur to him that he was wrong in oversimplifying the world order. Shutting up his grievance deep inside himself for years, he conceived the thought that he would someday be the judge between life and the dark forces which distort it, be life's champion and avenger.[6]

Strelnikov's fixation on Marxist principle, at the expense of an openness to life and humanity, sapped his revolution and drove it in the direction of nihilism. No man has the power, no matter where it is, to draw a line between life and oppression. Such a power is beyond revolution and ultimately works against it. (Revolution is instead the uprooting of death by the power of life.) Life itself resists the doctrinaire's program of judgment and fire; it will not surrender the justice of revolution to the injustice of means. The original power of the Revolution is maintained not in the ruthless idealism of Strelnikov, but in Zhivago who affirms, "Man is born to live, not to prepare for life. Life itself—the gift of life—is such a breathtakingly serious thing!"[7]

For the same reason it is not possible that revolution can be an instrument of ideology. Hungary and Vietnam proved that the two principal ideologies of the world have murder in their hearts. For any oppressed people to rely for their freedom on the assistance of a major state today is to risk involvement in corruption, deceit, and finally renewed suppression in the name of some exalted value that is visible only to their leaders.

Where is genuine revolution, revolution of resistance and of life, revolution which seeks peace by making peace? One finds the signs of a revolutionary power in man, not in mass movements and uprisings, but in persons, and even in those whose status in society is usually that of outcast and criminal. Before man can recognize the revolution of peace, he must recognize that truth fundamental to the works of Dostoevsky:

> Is the meaning of life buried so deep then that the wise man who perceives it can appear among us only as one misunderstood, only as a fool, the strong man who holds it in his hands, only as weak, the healthy man who draws his nourishment from it, only as sick? Is then the true interpretation, the meaning of all that happens on earth, so fully crowded out into the margin that only those who themselves are in some way out there—harlots, murderers, and the insane—can follow its trail and understand it? And that, wherever this meaning, this interpretation, is brought again into the center, it immediately seems to be a disruption of all that is customary—ridiculous naïveté, idiocy, something totally foreign, unprecedentedly different from everything that has previously happened and been thought?[8]

The revolution of peace proceeds from a recognition first of the need, and then of the power of those who are "crowded out into the margin" of the earth. Wisdom and power come not necessarily from the privileged but from those who know life from having found it in death, and light from having perceived it through the darkness. For those on the margin of the earth, most of the human race, need has given birth to power, but it is a power as yet unrealized and unexplored. One finds both the need and the power implicit in the recital of the life of a Sicilian laborer:

> Now I've got five sons. To earn enough to feed them, I worked both on the land and at sea, fishing at night and digging by day. For nearly all the summer, I'd never have more than three hours' sleep out of the twenty-four, and I led this sort of life for ten or twelve years, so that my hair was white by the time I was 35. I used to throw down the hoe in the street outside the house at five o'clock in the evening and be off to the fishing. We'd fish all night, although we were worn out by the work in the fields, and then in the morning we were off again ploughing. When we were at sea, we used to lie down on the seats of the boat and sleep while the nets were down, while the fish, the anchovies, were getting caught in them.[9]

The primary resource that the revolution has, by which it may transform a world of increasing suffering into a world of human respect, is in the depths of suffering itself. The weak have strength in their weakness and will learn to fight not with the guns of the powerful, but with the resources of their forged strength. What can change to make the native strength of the poor a primary and not merely an incidental factor in their struggle, and what will, on the other hand, deliver the powerful from the impotence of their weapons, is the emerging power of those who, without weapons, suffer for truth and justice and who appear to have no weapon at all. Suffering redeems and teaches the powerless something about life and about their very being which is capable of providing an enormous power against the oppressor. The seed of revolution is suffering: endurance is both the impulse and the potential strength of those who will rise up.

The native power of the weak over the apparently strong is evident in Vietnam, where the greatest military force in the world operating with ruthless efficiency has been unable to subdue a force of peasants. It has been said accurately that the object of war is to change the enemy's mind by making him suffer. Commander Stephen King-Hall formulated the normal logic of war as that of "bringing physical pressure to bear on the body so that its brain says: 'To avoid further misery I will give in and concede to the victor what he demands.' "[10] One presumes that a rise in the enemy's suffering will trigger an accelerating rising fear of further punishment and finally surrender. This general logic of war is dramatized in modern warfare, in which the strategy of massive land armies forcing surrender by occupation has given way to instant annihilation from the air. In the age of napalm, mass bombing, and nuclear weapons, the enemy is expected to be reasonable enough to surrender before his suffering has become literally inconceivable to us; or, to quote Herman Kahn's description, before the living envy the dead. The logic of war supposes that the suffering we can inflict by our weapons will defeat the enemy's mind and make him obedient to our will.

This logic of military power has been powerless against the kind of people the United States is fighting in Vietnam and will likely fight elsewhere. In addition to the powerful force's own corrupted idea they face the problem that the poor and the weak accept deep suffering as being of the very essence of life.[11] It is clear that we cannot assume that the enemy wishes to avoid death, pain, and material destruction enough to surrender. The poor and the weak know life itself is suffering. What is suffered in war by bombs has been suffered in peace by exploitation. What the rich only fear, the poor have suffered daily in Southeast Asia and have endured. William Pfaff has cited a Korean officer in South Vietnam as observing that Americans expect of life that they can be happy; Koreans and Vietnamese, he claimed, do not expect this.[12] The weak seem to have the power to endure the suffering they expect of life; as their suffering increases, their endurance is upheld and strengthened.

But if the weak have the power to endure suffering, and to that extent the power to revolt against the powerful, waging war confuses and compromises this power. When everybody commits atrocities, as in any war, everybody is provoked to justify further violence. When the weak wage revolution with the weapons of the powerful, they only justify the latter's more extensive and more efficient use of those weapons. To prevail and not simply to endure—to pit the power of the powerless directly against the weaknesses of the strong—the revolution of the poor must be informed and transformed by a power that identifies itself with suffering without being concomitantly limited by the uses of war; and thus it must be deeply present in pain and yet transcendent to retaliation.

Suffering is the matter of a crucified world and the flesh of its unrealized power; Love is its spirit and its life, the world's Power made real and the world's oppressed set free. Love is suffering divinized. Love is the world both crucified and overcoming.

The reality of a revolution of peace, obscure and compromised in the jungles of Vietnam, is found clear and radiant on certain roads of India. It is a reality present in the work of Vinoba Bhave, a follower of Gandhi, who remains almost unknown in the West despite his impact on the social structure of India.

Vinoba is the originator of the *Bhoodan-Gramdan* movement, which works to persuade the landowners of India, large and small, to surrender the bulk of their land to the poor and dispossessed. A seventy-three-year-old ascetic, Vinoba has for seventeen years been walking from village to village in India, accompanied by a growing number of followers and preaching the message of non-violence and *Bhoodan*. Bhoodan means "land gifts," and *gramdan* "village gifts." Yet it is not the pleasure of a gratuitous generosity, but a sense of the urgent requirements of justice, which Vinoba demands of his listeners. "I am not begging for alms," he says, "I am demanding what is owed to the poor." By 1962 Vinoba's campaign for the landless poor, which has spread from a one-man revolution to about 20,000 co-workers, had been given seven million acres for redistribution—still considerably short of his goal of 50 million acres, one-sixth of the peninsula's cultivable land and an area about the size of the whole of France. Vinoba's movement has since graduated to the concept of *gramdan*, the village in which enough land has been given to communize ownership in the village as a whole, and strong appeals have now begun to go out for district-*dan* and even state-*dan*. By August 1966 almost 25,000 villages had been secured and transferred from individual to communal ownership. This has all been accomplished without force or fear by a man who has never ridden in an automobile, yet who understands the meaning of power in the Nuclear Age.

The impossibility of his task is acknowledged by Vinoba in his interpretation of the movement's beginning. On April 18, 1951, at Pochampalli, when Vinoba had finished speaking to the people on peace, there was silence among them. Then some pariahs came forward and said, "We, too, love peace, but we are workers and have no land to work. What do you want us to do? Instead of talking to us about peace, give us land and we'll always live in peace."

Vinoba looked down, as though abashed, and was plunged in thought. Then, turning toward his audience, he cried, "There are some rich men among you and it is to them I am speaking now. You have been listening to my words of peace and you have all approved of them, it seems. Is it possible that none of you is willing to show that he has understood them, by relieving, say, the land famine from which these poor laborers are suffering?"

A man immediately stood up and offered one hundred acres. Those who had put forward their request only as a challenge were overwhelmed in the midst of the general astonishment.

"On that day," Vinoba says, "God gave me a sign. I meditated on it the whole of the following night and ended up by finding out what I had to do. . . .

"Without this hint on His part I should never have made up my mind to preach *Bhoodan,* so impossible did it seem to clever people to heal by this means one of the greatest sores of India and of the world. I should never have had the audacity for it, even if I'd had the idea.

"But I put my trust in Him. And even if my reason showed me that the task was an immense one, I felt that if I did not undertake it, my nonviolence would be shown up as only cowardice and good for nothing.

"That is why I received the Sign with gratitude and went forward with the adventure."[13]

Vinoba's adventure in nonviolence represents today a more living hope to the Indian poor than government programs or Marxist promises. He has had the inspiration to attack directly, with his marching feet and spirit, a problem which the Marxists claim can be solved only by violence. They have watched him sympathetically and jealously, incredulous at his success and skeptical of its continuation. One of them once said to him, "Your end is good, but your means are ridiculous. How can you hope to obtain great changes without using violence?"

"Tell me, my friend, did not a great change take place in you the day you became a Communist?"

"Yes, everything changed that day for me."

"But did you become a Communist of your own free will, or did someone force you with a gun to join the party?"

"What an idea! I read Marx, I found what he said true, and that is all there was to it."

"Then why do you think it impossible to obtain from others what Marx obtained from you?"[14]

Vinoba's question and the challenge of his revolution are as pertinent to Christianity as they are to Marxism. Neither has shown much faith in its ability to change men by the power of its truth. In the most crucial issues and conflicts, neither Marx nor Christ has been thought adequate by his followers to obtain from their opponents the same victory won over them. For the Christian, the contradiction raised by Vinoba—between a belief in the transforming power of truth and resort to violence because the truth is apparently powerless—seems a perversion of the life and teaching of Christ. It was Pilate, the man of violence, who asked despairingly, "What is truth?"

The crucifixion of the world that takes place from

Vietnam to Palma di Montechiaro must be seen in relation to both executioners and victims. Violence is the willed destruction of another, or, to use Simone Weil's phrase, the transformation of a man into a thing. To avoid the destitute is as violent an act as to repress them by guns and bombs.

The executioners of the world are not identifiable simply by wealth, position, or power; responsibility and guilt are not confinable to particular peoples. No man is free in conscience from the guilt of the executioner.

In the interaction of these two forces in the world—the force of violence and the force of suffering—the nature of true power is but gradually revealed in man's history. Power is revealed not as violence which destroys, nor even as suffering which endures, but as Truth which resists injustice through voluntary suffering and as Love which in suffering resistance opens the victim to the executioner and transforms their relationship from that of objects, passive and active, to that of persons, confronted and confronting. In the confrontation of violence by Truth and Love, the activity of violence is revealed as passive and futile and the passivity of suffering unfolds as active and overcoming. From this confrontation power is seen as the ability to redeem from inhumanity both victim and executioner.

Faith in the power of Truth is not abstract or idealistic but deeply incarnational, a faith lived in human suffering and death, but turned toward life and an open tomb. The incarnation of Truth is found in the dust raised by the sandaled feet of Vinoba and his followers, whose humble way is necessary to serve the poor and truly represent their need. Truth can exert its enormous power only by being incarnated in the humility and apparent weakness of suffering Love, a Love which therefore raises no obstacles to Truth by violence, but on the contrary, affirms the other's existence at its very base by service and sacrifice, and opens him to dialogue with the confronter. Truth is powerless without suffering Love as its medium. Given that medium, however, Truth takes hold in men as the power to raise them from the death of injustice and war to the life of community.

The revolution of peace has taken hold also in the land of Palma di Montechiaro, in northwest Sicily, home of the Mafia and site of the most violent and corrupt social milieu in Western Europe. In the "triangle of hunger," which bred the famous bandit Giuliano, the nonviolent revolution of Danilo Dolci has begun to work changes in a society with virtually a stone-age ethos.

Dolci is a forty-four-year-old former student of architecture whose campaigns for justice on behalf of the hungry of Sicily have combined the talents of sociologist, publicist, relief worker, and follower of Gandhi. Since 1952 when he moved from northern Italy to live with the Sicilian poor, Dolci has kept up a sustained protest against the inhuman conditions prevailing under a corrupt power alliance of the Mafia and the Christian Democratic government and supported by the Church in Sicily. What began as a personal crusade has expanded through Dolci's books, broadcasts, demonstrations, and fasts into a community of volunteer workers. The community has been organized by Dolci into cells, each built around an agro-technician and a welfare group, which have been sent out to establish centers in the most desperately deprived areas and live under the constant threat of violence. Their purpose is to stimulate local employment and encourage a consciousness of self-help. Each worker was to be, in Dolci's words, "a moral reference point" in an area of 430,000 inhabitants which has only four people with degrees in agriculture, no competent authority concerned with education or sociology, and where there is an average of one murder every five days.[15] It is this work and the conditions which prompted it, as described in Dolci's book *To Feed the Hungry*, that was a direct source of inspiration for President Kennedy's founding of the Peace Corps.

In September 1962 Dolci underwent a sustained fast as an appeal to the Italian government for the building of a dam essential to the area's development. He fasted until the ninth day when, as his health took a dangerous turning point, the government agreed to begin work on the dam within five months. Dolci warned officials that he would fast again if there were delays, and the work on the dam began, as promised.

A year later Dolci fasted for another large dam. On the tenth day of the fast the government pledged it would build it. As a result of these two fasts, but above all, of the truth and love expressed through the man who suffered them, the people of Sicily will soon be served by an irrigation network that will be the envy of larger states.

Dolci has often been called ingenuous and a dreamer. He replies, "I'd say that he who hasn't yet understood that the discovery of truth is the strongest force of all, he's the ingenuous one, he's the dreamer."[16]

Dolci's revolution is rooted in the people, whose life he shares and whose hopes he has organized into a nonviolent attack against the structure of injustice. "There is God in these people," he has written, "like the fire that smoulders under the ashes." "This land is like one of the many beautiful little girls you see in the alleys of its townships. The beauty is often there beneath the scabs, the raving hair, the wild and tattered rags: and already you can picture what an appearance of graphic and noble intelligence a good upbringing would give to those features. . . ."[17]

It was this deeply lived vision and faith that prompted a friend to say of Dolci: "Danilo transforms others. It's a kind of moral strength which can transform even politics."[18]

To ask if transformation of man is a historical possibility is to ask whether man himself is a continuing historical possibility. For it is clear that man as he has thus far shaped and understood himself, and as he is confronted by nuclear power and global misery, has remaining only the future symbolized in the Book of Revelation. The transformation of politics is not merely a subject for meditation or for theological debate, but a mandate of conscience for every man who lies awake in an age of suffering.

But when resistance to suffering Love rises in a backlash of fear and strikes down the prophet of nonviolence, as America struck down Martin Luther King, the power of transformation becomes a power of judgment—if not judgment by fire then by fear and inner sterility. Transformation continues in the midst of fear and pushes back the threats of the blind. If in the end the sword is still taken, only the one who takes it perishes. Love and its community remain.

It is true of the suffering poor who fill the earth that there is God in these people—like the fire that smolders under the ashes. There is no God other than that Fire. If God appears dead in the Nuclear Age, it is because he has not been sufficiently liberated from his bondage in suffering man—the presence of God in mankind is above all the presence of man crucified. And this presence is dimly seen and scarcely felt when the crucified are crowded out onto the margin of the earth. God lives where men are beaten and die, but He lives to bring them and their murderers to life, and His life comes to life only when He emerges from them as Truth and as Love. The life of God is the life of the crucified, but while He is deeply present in crucifixion the unveiling of His presence is in resurrection, a resurrection which can be seen and felt only by those in whom Love and Truth have taken hold. God is dead where men lie dying and unseen. He lives where crucifixion is seen and felt and entered into, as neither victim nor executioner but as Love suffering and as Truth overcoming. Crucifixion becomes redemptive precisely when the victim recognizes his divinity. Man takes that step when he responds to injustice with Love, with suffering, resistant, and overpowering. Man becomes God when Love and Truth enter into man, not by man's power but raising him to Power, so that revolution in Love is revealed finally as the Power of resurrection.

To join the revolution of peace is to enter the Fire smoldering under the ashes of men suffering and to feel the intensity of its promise. It is to discover that Fire rising already into flame at the beginning of the greatest revolution in history. The Fire of Truth and Love rising from the ashes and restoring the ashes to flame is the only power remaining in the Nuclear Age. To enter that Fire is to become one with God in man, as God has revealed himself in such servants of man as Gandhi, Vinoba, and Dolci, and as Pope John, Dag Hammarskjöld, and U Thant. The revolution of peace is the rising flame of man daring to become truly human, the flame of man beginning to live with himself without fear. It is a Fire which has only begun in man and which will end only when it has burned his image from earth into the heavens, transfiguring man into the God who is his Power.

NOTES

1. Arata Osada, *Children of the A-Bomb* (New York: G. P. Putnam's Sons, 1963), pp. 151-52.
2. J. D. Bernal, "The Human Family: A Map of Need," in Walter Stein (ed.) *Peace on Earth: The Way Ahead* (London: Sheed and Ward, 1966), p. 62.
3. Dr. B. R. Sen of FAO made the first half of this statement during the week of October 16, 1966, as quoted by Louis B. Fleming in the *Vancouver Sun*, October 27, 1966. As U.S. forces in Vietnam rise to 550,000, the estimate of $30 billion a year as the American cost of the war may even be low. The significance of this figure is evident in the fact that one year of the Peace Corps is equal to the cost of 32 hours of the Vietnam War.
4. Danilo Dolci, *Waste* (London: Macgibbon & Kee, 1963), p. 15.
5. Bernal, p. 66.
6. Boris Pasternak, *Doctor Zhivago* (Fontana Books, 1965), p. 248.
7. Pasternak, p. 292.
8. Eduard Thurneysen, *Dostoevsky*, trans. by Keith R. Crim (John Knox Press, 1964), p. 27.
9. Danilo Dolci, *The Outlaws of Partinico* (London: Macgibbon & Kee, 1960), pp. 168-69.
10. Stephen King-Hall, *Defense in the Nuclear Age* (Nyack, N.Y.: Fellowship Publications, 1959), p. 31. King-Hall also believed, however, that an enemy's mind could be changed by an appeal to reason and that nonviolent methods are the only effective defense in the Nuclear Age.
11. For this point I am indebted to a short but penetrating article by William Pfaff, "The Strategy of the Weak," *Commonweal*, July 22, 1966, pp. 456-67. Felix Greene developed the same point in a series of articles for *The Vancouver Sun* after he returned from three months in North Vietnam. See especially his "Paradox of 'Bombed-Out' North Viet Nam: People Strong Because They're Poor," *The Vancouver Sun*, July 6, 1967.
12. Pfaff, p. 457.
13. This account and Vinoba's comments are drawn from Lanza del Vasto, *Gandhi to Vinoba: The New Pilgrimage* (London: Rider and Company, 1956), p. 85.
14. Del Vasto, pp. 171-72.

15. The details about Dolci's workers are given in an excellent biography: *Fire Under the Ashes: The Life of Danilo Dolci* by James McNeish (London: Hodder and Stoughton, 1965), p. 163.
16. McNeish, p. 156.
17. McNeish, pp. 68, 169.
18. McNeish, p. 217.

THE HUMAN REVOLUTION: A SEARCH FOR WHOLENESS

George W. Morgan

Man is the questionable being. He lives in possibility. He hovers between realization and failure. He is the being of reason and lack of reason, of speech and inarticulateness; the being of truth and falsehood, justice and its denial, love and estrangement.

"Who am I?" is a question that can have no fixed and definite answer; sometimes it can be a terrible question. The question, "Who are you?" can welcome and call me forth, beckon and sustain me, or it can refuse and destroy.

At every moment of his existence man may be affirmed or denied, his humanness acknowledged or ignored, and the wholeness of his being fostered or maimed. Today there is much that maims.

It is true that there are innumerable activities and institutions that are devoted to human welfare: alleviation of poverty, famine, disease; protection and development of the individual through democracy and education. But despite these achievements, and often in their midst, man as man is being denied, not only in that much poverty, for example, still exists in the world and little is generally done about it, or in that many men in this land that says it prizes freedom and opportunity are deprived of elementary rights. Even among the privileged, in the warp and woof of modern life, man is denied.

We do not really concern ourselves with man. We concern ourselves with isolated interests. We are intent, for example, on increasing the speed of everything. We take for granted that since speed is sometimes desirable, more speed is always more desirable—the speed of travel, for instance. If it is possible to build airplanes that hurtle us from place to place at twice or five times the speed they do now, then it at once seems imperative to build them. What will this do to the traveler? What will it do to the soul to annihilate distance? What will it mean to be torn from one culture and almost instantly dropped in another, to have increased fivefold the already harrowing rate of experience? What will it do to those on the ground whose small remnant of quiet will be totally shattered by sonic boom? What could be done to enhance human life if the enormous effort and cost were directed to other ends?

Goals and pursuits seem beyond the pale of assessment. There is incessant change, but no consideration of the merit of these self-perpetuating interests. The change is for "progress" and "efficiency," where progress is expansion in size and increase in rate of whatever it may be, and efficiency is smoothness of internal operation, subordination of everything to the isolated aim. We produce more and more things and because surfeit is the inevitable result continuously contrive new ones. We take it for granted that sixteen years (at least) of attendance in schools—a process we optimistically call "education"—is a human necessity, if not the gate to salvation, and try to push everyone through an efficient mill to get his diploma. We think knowledge and the search for knowledge are an unmitigated good and hence stuff our minds with information and news, conduct frantic research into everything, and amass print at a staggering pace.

Technology, education, and knowledge have a place in human life, an important place. There are many claims and demands upon us. Man has the power and burden of assessment and decision. He is the being who can say yes and no—who *must*, to keep his humanity. By renouncing assessment and clinging to prevailing goals, we avoid having to face the difficult and often disturbing questions of human existence. We hide from the recognition that many of the activities and goals we accept and to which we contribute are worthless or destructive.

In almost every area of modern society the human being is subordinated to systems. Mechanisms constitute the chief model for thought and practice. Standardization and routinization rule our lives.

The sheer weight of numbers, of course, pushes us in that direction. The more mouths to be fed, houses to be built, pupils to be taught, and patients to be examined, the greater the pressure to mechanize and systematize.

This is the easiest way to deal with large demand. Industrial mass production, with its stupendous results, has become the pattern for office, store, social service, hospital, and school. But there is not only the problem of numbers and the weight of industrial influence. Mechanisms and systems are also tempting. They serve single and definite goals; the problems with which they present us have clearcut solutions; they allow us to look away from the complexity of actual men and the ambivalences of real situations; they provide us with ready-made answers to all questions and with prompt appeasement of all doubts.

Just as speed, power, and knowledge, moreover, so systematization and standardization are regarded as independent, self-justifying goals. We do not ask where they are desirable and where not; the question cannot be posed from within the system—it requires a vision with larger scope.

Indiscriminate standardization and obsession with efficient procedure imprison man. They assign him to a role, insert him in a slot, push him through channels. The more fixed and smooth the operation, the more life is laid out in grooves and the less room remains for actual men.

Man's work is deprived of meaning; it is reduced to the bare business of earning a living.

What differences are there between this and meaningful work? To make a significant part of an object has more meaning than to make over and over the same insignificant fragment. To have intimate contact with wood or stone has more meaning than to handle memos or dials. To work with tools that grow to fit the shape of a man's hand, whose touch and use he knows so that they become like friends, has more meaning than to work with things that forever remain alien. To produce or sell what men need has more meaning than to produce or sell what one must talk men into believing they need. To have a relation of person and person with others with whom one works or for whom one makes an object or renders a service has more meaning than to be inserted in an utterly impersonal process without contact with others, or else with contact that forces one into being a replaceable bearer of a standardized function, so that personal presence becomes interruption. Systems, machines, and standard routines are often the best, quickest, and most efficient way of getting things done. But the question is, What is it that ought to get done? Work must be considered in the total context of human life. Even the product of our work is rarely considered with respect to all that it means or might mean to man—think of the enormous resistance, for example, to giving attention to minimal safety of the automobile. But even when the product is more fully considered, such consideration is not yet enough. There is also the question of the human task. The product is only the end of the act of producing, and this act is a large and vital part of our lives.

This is not a sentimental plea for return to "romantic" conditions or a Golden Age. It is, on the contrary, an acknowledgment of all the reality that modern society, obsessed with its goals and techniques, forever ignores.

We have tried to offset the meaninglessness of work by looking for fulfillment in leisure. But this is a misguided solution. It knows nothing of the joy of work and of work that is central to the realization of life. It mistakes the present degraded nature of work for its essence. At best this solution means that leisure is devoted to the kind of meaningful activity that work should also be, and that life is split in two, with the larger part condemned. At worst, and most often, it means that leisure is nothing but escape from the deadening routine of work and that an even more deadening boredom lies like a leaden weight on the hours of leisure. Modern society supplies countless means to kill time. Can there be a more terrible sickness than this deliberate denial of human existence, this poisonous feeling that the short and precarious span allotted to man is too long, this ceaseless search for spiritual death in the midst of physical health?

Many today anticipate the automation revolution. They speak of it in glowing terms: At last, they say, man will be free. But what, we must ask, will he be free for? Will he simply be free for more hours of boredom? Will he have to kill his whole life?

Some, it is true, think of leisure in higher and more acceptable terms. They think of books, of the pursuit of knowledge, of art. They have before them the image of men in the past whose privileged economic and social position allowed them freedom to think and read and write. With machines to do our work, to provide our food and clothing, our shelter and furnishings and other necessaries of life, we will all be free for science, poetry, and painting.

But this vision stems from a badly distorted and unrealistic view of man. Unrealistic, most obviously, because it neglects the fact that works of science and poems are not used or consumed as are shirts or food. We do not need millions of men to do research in physics; we do not need millions of poems. Not only is there no need of them; it would be disastrous to have them. For human sharing is essential to these realms. Already humanity suffers critically from a fragmentation of culture; already it is so submerged in the explosive quantity of knowledge and art that almost all have abandoned the attempt to gain some unified vision of man's existence and to participate in the life of a true community of men. To multiply these things will seal the disaster.

But even apart from contributing to more science and art, even if most men's leisure were devoted to reading or seeing what others have done, this view of life is distorted. It lifts learning and art clear out of the context of human life as a whole and sets them apart in a vacuum, ignoring the point that they are effete when divorced from a fullness of life. The view accepts the current condition of self-justifying pursuits and drives it further. It ignores the fact that there is a gulf between study that answers to living questions and study that stems from idle curiosity.

What man does has meaning when it answers a call. We have forgotten entirely the old meaning of following a "calling." Though we may not be able to hear a summons from God, there can still be a summons from the world if we but ready ourselves to listen. Wherever we find a life, whether exalted or humble, that can serve as inspiration to others, it is the life of one who saw that there was something he had to do, was meant to do, and who stood in vital relation to the world, his historical situation, and a human community.

We must use our technology not to eliminate work, but to humanize it. In other times and places men often had—and still have—great difficulty in providing for their elementary needs. We can readily understand why they were chiefly concerned to ease this crushing burden. But our situation is different. Our problem is not production, but overproduction. We do not have to chain ourselves to mechanization and standardization to keep alive. On the contrary, if we consider their place in the totality of life and use them properly, we can now allow men to do work that has meaning and to make products more suitable for human life. We can fit the machine and the system to humans. We can make place for a new kind of craftsmanship that makes judicious use of modern technology. Genuine attention can be given to quality of product and service, and standardization can be used in a setting of personal presence. And we will not deplore but welcome the attendant reduction in the mass of largely meretricious products that now suffocate and cloy us.

How does the individual live his life in the midst of the institutions and systems of modern time? Why does he do whatever he does? What does he look for and hope for?

The effort to live the good life through material possession and consumption has long since reached the grotesque. The old materialist obsession with having and using is pathetic enough; more pathetic still is the new one, which mainly consists in acquiring and discarding. No sooner has something been bought than interest fades; the interval between a thing's newness and oldness is close to zero; obsolescence all but overtakes invention.

How often we hear the word "fun." How often people do what they do, or say they do what they do, because they enjoy it. Quite possibly they do not always believe this; they may have other reasons for their actions, which they either cannot admit to themselves or are unable or reluctant to express. But the significant fact remains that it is taken for granted that fun and enjoyment are adequate grounds for whatever one does.

Certainly it is important to do things that provide enjoyment. But fun cannot be the aim that shapes man's life. If all is "enjoyed," one will not know true joy.

What gives rise to this shallow hedonism? Is it not that we find ourselves in an atmosphere in which meanings are lacking? Is this philosophy of fun not a philosophy of barrenness and estrangement? If we are immersed in systems and practices that are never questioned in depth, especially perhaps because they are often so dubious, then we give up looking for meaning. We look for a place in the system and are content to find that this place provides fun. Fun is harmless, we say, and society agrees. We make no claim that what we do has importance, and appear quite modest to ourselves.

But it is a pseudo-modesty; if questioned, we are likely to be very proud of it. It is a veil society offers us for hiding from ourselves and from the world that might call us. We take refuge in the assertion of a strictly private satisfaction because we shy away from the knowledge that nothing vital relates us to others, our culture, and mankind.

The subordination of the person to impersonal systems denies him the sense of potency. He does not feel himself as a being who can initiate significant action. He cannot make himself heard. Feeling this negation of his humanity, the individual looks for ways to assert it. He needs to prove his potency and gain attention for himself; he wants to do things that would not be if it were not for him—he craves self-affirmation.

Originality seems to fulfill this need. This is why we praise it so often and pursue it so constantly. But the pursuit of originality is spurious self-affirmation, a deceiving substitute for genuine human existence, and it usually proceeds within the mold of established goals and organizations. If one questions the goals and organizations and points to basic change, deep renewal, he generally encounters inertia and stony deafness. The new is valued as long as it doesn't make fundamental demands—hence, it is not really new. People acquire it or are "interested" in it, but go on their way fundamentally untouched.

In this manner, room has even been made for a newness that in some respects reacts against, even vehemently against, the prevalent order. Artistic originality, for example, is applauded for its own sake, not only when the artist himself has sought nothing else and has looked only for self-assertion, but also when his work has real significance and even when it implies the destruction of much of what his society stands for; this applause allows the impact of the work to be neutralized and its significance avoided.

Every act that stems from true personal being has an element of newness; every real decision, every genuine answer to a genuine question, involves originality. But when genuine human life is absent, such new acts and original answers are replaced by the search for originality and newness as such. What is done then no longer matters: the meaning of the act is ignored; the truth of the answer, the significance of the decision, fade away. The gaze is upon one's self because this self is so radically denied, and the new and original—whatever they are—are seized on as means to affirm the self. But it can not be affirmed in this way. The affirmation is momentary and delusive, and so one rushes on again in yet another search for the "new."

So much of our existence is devoid of meaning; so much is deadly routine; so many vital parts of our being are denied and suppressed. We are taught to disavow our feelings and sensibilities, and therefore we are estranged from them. Our prevailing systems of knowledge—based on science and areas influenced by science—because they tend to be rigidly rational, lead us to distrust personal commitment. Our systems of practice—technology, industry, and standardized organization—exclude it. Our distorted and guilty view of our bodies (which has not been basically changed by the sexual revolution) reduces and poisons our awareness of our own bodily sensations. We do not sense ourselves present in our experience and do not sense ourselves as initiators of our own actions. We go through activities that a system imposes upon us. We play roles. We ourselves are divorced from what we do—so consistently divorced that we end up not knowing who we are and even wondering if there *is* a we, if we are not only the sequence of motions we go through. (And various influential theoretical interpretations in psychology and sociology tell us that this is indeed so.)

Small wonder that we are always in search of excitement to rouse us from boredom. We become stimulated, something is happening. Our feelings leap up, our bodies tingle, a thrill passes through us. We seem to be doing something that is our own doing.

Excitement alone, however, is a substitute, a reaction against the state of nonbeing. Our incessant movement, our search for novelty, and our obsession with speed are all ways of seeking excitement. Anything and everything will serve: jetting to London, cruises to exotic lands, new fashions, sexual experiments in groups, drugs, contrived shocks in the arts and at social gatherings.

Our institutions and systems accommodate this urge, and even people who protest the systems tend to be infected with the same impulse—a tendency that is reinforced each time genuine protest receives no hearing. Activism takes the place of significant action and excitement becomes the surrogate.

Modern man looks for the fulfillment of life in his own private being. This is the complement of the absence of true human existence. Boundless assertion of private interest goes hand in hand with renunciation of assessment of public institutions and goals. Intense concern with the self is the obverse of subordination of the self in the dominant structures.

Man is possibility that awaits fulfillment. Humanness may be realized or maimed. But its realization is not *self*-realization, for humanness does not reside in the "I."

Human existence is existence with a world. Relation to the world is man's essential possibility. Not a relation of whatever kind between one thing and another, nor a relation of mastering, acquiring, or using, though that, too, is required, but relation precisely in its most distinctively human sense.

What it is cannot be adequately described. One can only point to it as one takes another by the hand and points to something he must see for himself. Relation is something that occurs between an I and an Other. It is neither in me nor in the Other, nor is it always there when I and the Other are together, in proximity or interaction. But it may be there. The Other can be the maple tree I see from the window of the room in which I write, or the squirrels that frolic on the bare branches, or the book I read a little while ago, or the person who may knock at my door any moment. My relation with each of these is very different from my relations with the others. But something essential is common to all. I am aware of an Other which claims me and to which I respond. This Other is really other—not simply an ingredient of my environment, but a being of its own. I am open to its presence. I am touched by it, struck by it, not only glancingly, but in my center.

The relation with another person is potentially the fullest of all man's relations with the world, and the most central. It is the only one which allows complete mutuality, in which another is open to my presence as I am to his. If we *are* open to each other, then each is allowed to come forth, to disclose himself, to affirm who he is in truth. Demand and opportunity are joined—each person is called on and each is welcomed. Both are present in being present to each other in reciprocal address and answer—address and answer that are not always in words.

Full mutuality is rarely experienced. Often an address is not really heard, and the answer is not really an answer. Or the answer, though truly an answer, is not accepted because it touches parts of oneself that have been disavowed. Often one or both persons are far from being able to listen to the other and to be truly themselves. But full mutuality is the peak of the relation of man with man by which all other relation—to the extent it is genuine—is guided.

Relation between man and world is never without difficulty and is always endangered. But modern life seems almost to conspire against it. We do not encounter the world; we are unable to be present to whatever it may be that arises to meet us. We seek only to dominate and to use, and we approach the world armed with formula and program. With these we get hold of everything and reduce it to manageable form, inserting it in categories and systems and stripping it of singularity and strangeness. We want everything calculated and subjected to standard techniques. We want to predict and control.

All this is necessary, of course. Men are threatened by the world and must protect themselves, they have to gain mental and practical mastery to maintain existence, they have to use things for food and shelter. And precisely because it is necessary, it readily overwhelms everything else. Domination and use are not comprised in a totality of life in which they would cease to be mere domination and use and become material of true human existence: they *are* life.

This means that there is no true present. We do not allow anything to arise from the midst of an actual encounter and are not ready for what cannot be foreseen, what is born in the spontaneousness of real presence. We are not open to anything that cannot be disposed of and handled by our methods of explanation and manipulation. We neutralize and subdue—and remain fixed, closed, and untouched. We do not hear ourselves addressed because we do not listen. We are not aware of an Other because we refuse its own being.

Genuine response to an Other cannot be planned. It is the very substance of the existence of a unique being. Something confronts him, and everything depends on his being ready—ready to be present. What is wanted is not a stock reply, a routine act, or a calculated move, but the person himself. If he truly answers, it is a creative answer; it arises here and now in the secret instant of unrepeatable meeting.

Modern life tends to exclude such creative answer, and its notion of creativeness therefore ignores the world. To be creative, we think, is to bring forth from the solitary self. And what we expect from human creation—not surprisingly—is no less than the world. Scientists, businessmen, and politicians speak in this way. And there are even those who speak of human existence in terms of each man's inhabiting his own world, the world *he* has created, and he is said to create his own self too, and also values and meanings. We hear it from artists and educators, philosophers and psychotherapists.

We are so intent on creation because we are so deprived of true relation with the world. If the I is without genuine relation to the Other, it becomes preoccupied with itself. When it is cut off from the meaning of call and answer, it falls into the illusion of being itself the solitary creator of meaning and world.

Our attitude toward creation shows how desperately we are caught on the horns of a false dilemma. On the one hand, we want to make everything, we want to be pure creators. We want to see ourselves as beings who are capable of originating in total independence. On the other, we want everything explained and controlled, and refuse to admit that there is anything that cannot be subsumed in our systems—including creation. And so we try to explain and produce it according to formula. We even claim that it lies in the scope of electronic computers—those programmed products of our systems of science and technology.

We oscillate between the two equally nonhuman alternatives of being "creators" and being results, being utterly autonomous and being nothing but products.

Modern life is essentially oblivious of relation between man and man, the social is widely mistaken for the interhuman;[1] the fact that men live in society, depend on each other, and interact with each other is supposed to constitute human relationship. But it does not. Even ants do all this. "Group activity" is no assurance that people are truly present to each other. Isolation is nowhere more frequent than at parties. How revealing it is that words of intimate human relation are applied now in places where essentially no such relation exists: the government, business, and university "family"; the factory that is the "home" of its product; the letters from advertisers that begin "Dear Friend."

Our life with each other is predominantly functional; it is inserted into standardized grooves. We do not meet as person and person, but as embodied functions. We do not regard others as concrete individuals engaged in a task, but see them defined by the task. We reduce them to their social "roles." And most of our theoretical study of human society not only echoes this view but takes for granted that role playing *is* human relation. But all this is separated by a gulf from mutual presence.

Even apart from our major routines, we are not ready for meeting. We are not open to an Other, but insert him in concepts and explain him. We "figure him out" with our favorite psychology, sociology, or cybernetics, using these weapons to protect ourselves from an impact, from being called on to face what cannot be manipulated at will. We turn with eagerness to the conceptualizations offered by sciences or by studies emulating them, not only because they have prestige, but also because they give us the illusion of having hold of everything, being "on top" of every situation. We have allowed the attitude of conquest and control, which so largely informs science and technology, to become the sole way of life. We even deliberately try to convert every province of social existence into a kind of engineering. Education, for example, has been said to be a branch of technology,[2] and much "progress" in education, from the use of methods derived from behavioristic psychology (which explicitly regards man under the category of mechanism) to the "teaching machine," consists precisely in engineering men. And the proliferation of fields called social engineering, human engineering, decision mathematics, and so on show how radically we have lost sight of what constitutes true relation between men, and how utterly unaware we are that such relation is the heart of human existence.

Our social fabric militates against relation. Competitiveness pervades everything we do and is taught from the time we are small children. Work and play are conceived as contest and race. Tests and ratings of aptitudes and achievements incessantly compare us and pit us against each other. Debates are staged for political and intellectual rivalry. We seize on the half-truth that competition forces everyone to do his best (*half*-truth, because this best is by no means always the best in human terms) and completely ignore what this does to human meeting. Our fundamental stance is not to respond to others, but to outdo them, vie with them, beat them. Aggressiveness is praised, the "go-getter" is admired. At the same time, we naïvely believe that universal brotherhood springs magically from this Darwinian struggle. And we are helped in this delusion by the veneer of "friendliness," "personnel," "public," and even "human relations" that now covers the pervasive strife.

It is impossible in such a context to entrust oneself to another. Truth in the area of human relation is the true disclosure of oneself. (This does not mean self-exhibition, of course, or neglect of essential delicacy, patience, and tact.) How can you disclose yourself in a life of incessant rivalry? You cannot. On the contrary, you learn to dissemble. You do what you think is likely to help you achieve your specific purpose: you pose, play roles, do what is expected so as to smooth your path. And, of course, you expect the other to do the same. Both are steeped in mutual distrust; neither expects the other to be truthful, to be himself, to be genuinely present.

True relation is not the same as love. Love is the utmost relation. Something much less but crucial is required in all our life. It is one's acknowledgment of the other as person, the particular person he is. To acknowledge him is to recognize that he, too, is human, capable of the joy and beset by the burden of humankind. It is to regard him not as a thing of interest or use to oneself, but as Other. He can and must be regarded this way even in the most brief and routine transaction. He can be acknowledged in the instant his face emerges and confronts one in a crowd. He can be acknowledged when one's own aims and his are opposed.

Acknowledgment affirms the other's existence, it allows and enables him to be. For man is not fixed and settled, nor is he complete unto himself. What he is is essentially what he is in relation. Acknowledgment by another is confirmation of his being.

Lack of acknowledgment is the chief reason for modern man's deep insecurity and obsessive search for reassurance. Sometimes this search takes the path of total insertion in a group, of self-erasure by conformity and "adjustment." Sometimes it is the twofold attempt to confirm himself directly by aggression or "creativity," and simultaneously, to wrest confirmation from others in the form of attention or applause.

True confirmation cannot be found in these ways. Neither by hiding nor inflating himself can man truly realize his life. Genuine selfhood is found in the act of reciprocal acknowledgment of man by man. Men give and receive their being in mutual response.

Most of the modern studies of man that have pervasive influence on our thought and action essentially follow the point of view and method of the sciences of inanimate matter. They take it for granted that the whole can be divided without loss into parts. They reduce the complex to the simple, the developed to the primitive, the higher to the lower, the unified to the divided. The modern specialist tends to allow the part he has focused on to displace the rest. Imprisoned by the false notion that science is the only way of knowledge, awed by the success of the physical sciences and the power they yield, and often, it would seem, reacting against the traditional view of man as made in the image of God or as endowed with a soul, which he can no longer accept, he is determined to pull man down —to the white rat, a physicochemical process, a mechanism, a mere result.

The way we live our lives joins with these views. Fed into the hopper[3] of a standard process, man is reduced to a product. Subjected to the machine, he becomes an automaton. Even where human qualities are still more in evidence, there is little room for the whole human being. We recognize only technicians and experts.

How conventional it is to cleave man into reason and emotion, and to extol the first and defame the second. With man's spirit thus fatally dismembered, reason is reduced to narrow intellect and pragmatic know-how. Emotion is suppressed as baleful, but since this suppression is not fully successful, means are provided for release. The search for excitement of which I spoke earlier is a desperate attempt to escape from the prevalent deadness, a frenzied desire to *feel.* And just as a man who is dying of thirst will drink even polluted water, so one who is dying from lack of emotion will do anything to regain it. No wonder the manifestations of emotion we see today so frequently take the forms of infantilism or violence.

One cannot see man without seeing him whole.[4] The primary meaning of being an individual is to be indivisible. If the whole is displaced by a part or divided into compartments, it is maimed. The whole man denies no part of himself; he acknowledges and unifies all elements of human existence. His reason and feeling, power and weakness, hopes and fears, and many desires are all in communion with each other. He is *a* being, a unified being.

Every decision and action arises from his whole self. He does not seek to escape from the inevitable tensions of life by mutilation. It is *he* who is present in whatever he does. He does not disintegrate his being into a series of roles, or amputate any facet of himself to fit a function.

To be "I" is to be *one,* in touch with every corner and layer of myself. To know *who* I am is to know one being: many-faceted, complex, aware of numerous and often conflicting claims, incapable of meeting all and therefore required to decide and to sacrifice, standing in different relations to different people—son and husband, teacher and thinker, friend and colleague, and so on, to all the manifoldness and contrasts of life: all this, yet *one.*

The more whole a person, the more capable he is of

relation, especially of relation with another person. Only in wholeness can one be truly present. Only if every region of the self can be touched is it possible to be open to the other and really to hear him. Only if one's own limitations and doubts can be faced, can one allow the other to disclose himself, for only then is one not in need of defenses and walls—dissemblance and pretense—but ready for the uniqueness of the other's being, ready to live this moment of true life.

At the same time, the more fully one lives in relation, the more whole is one's self. For it is the world that calls and elicits one's human potentials. It is in true presence that these potentials are unified. It is another's response that confirms one's existence.

Wholeness is never complete or final. Each new situation addresses us anew and calls for true answer. Often we fail to be wholly present; often we are not confirmed. But the sense of wholeness can more and more fully inform our lives.

A society aware of wholeness would not elevate special goals above human existence. It would not pursue profit, knowledge, expansion, or any interest as if it were the only one. It would reject the idea that every institution is law and purpose unto itself, realizing that such arrogant institutions are bound to distort humanity. Such a society would know that neither business nor politics, neither science nor art, may shelve the questions of human good. It would know that such cupboard morality, brought out for display on special occasions, is immorality.

One means to overcome the destruction inherent in our

insular aims and self-perpetuating institutions is an all-encompassing system in which everything is foreseen, planned, and prescribed. But such a supersystem, while ending the heedless assertion of isolated interests, would only make more uniform and efficient what the current systems already accomplish—the fragmentation and mutilation of man. It would insert us as cogs in one vast machine, and destroy the humanity it was supposed to guard.

The way to realize man is really a *way,* not a system. It is the way each one must take as a man who seeks to be whole. It is the way of relation.

A radical transformation is demanded of our time, a revolution for the sake of the humanity of man, a revolution against all those elements of current life that distort and destroy man. The where and when of this transformation are each here and now. It will require institutional changes—economic, political, educational, intellectual, and so on—but no merely institutional change will do. The essence of the change is toward a life of wholeness and relation, and this human revolution cannot be accomplished by external measures, nor will measures uninformed by wholeness and relation do anything other than continue or hasten our crisis.

What is demanded, moreover, cannot be accomplished once and for all. We do not realize humanness by the establishment of a fixed state, but by a way we must take each mortal hour with all our being. The sense of this way is present, I believe, in every man. Though often obscured and betrayed, it is a way each one can glimpse whenever he is ready to be truly touched by the world.

Could it be that this is how we, who live in an age of

the "eclipse of God,"[5] are still called by God and summoned to His way even though we are not aware of Him?

NOTES

1. This distinction has been made by Martin Buber. The difference between the two realms is explored in "Elements of the Interhuman," trans. by Ronald Gregor Smith, in Martin Buber, *The Knowledge of Man,* edited with an introduction by Maurice Friedman (New York, 1965).
2. See B. F. Skinner, "The Technology of Education," in *Cumulative Record* (New York, 1959).
3. This phrase is not mine but that of a man prominent in educational circles who recently used it in a speech at Brown University in describing an efficient system of graduate education that he would like to see established.
4. For a fuller exploration of wholeness and related themes, see the author's *The Human Predicament: Dissolution and Wholeness* (Providence, R.I.: Brown University Press, 1968).
5. Martin Buber, *The Eclipse of God,* trans. by Maurice Friedman *et al.* (New York, 1952).

THE RACE REVOLUTION: REFLECTIONS ON A DYING REPUBLIC

(Dedicated to Rudolph Nathaniel Gordon, Jr.)

William Strickland

In modern times, the American republic sits astride the world. It is the mightiest land. Yet, its might is without grace; its power, without compassion. It is, we are told, self-righteously, "the champion of freedom everywhere." Its citizenry, taught not to think but to believe, nods in assent and seems untroubled by the fact that their country has exterminated and enslaved two races, the Indian and the African, and now wages cruel warfare against a third, the Vietnamese. Neither discrepancies nor horrors unsettle them.

There are many things askew in America. Overshadowing them all is a kind of infectious dishonesty. Margaret Halsey has called America "the lying society." Lying has become a more pervasive aspect of the way we live than affluence. Not everybody in America is affluent, but everybody gets lied to. And when the lies are found out ("We have not bombed Hanoi"), it is not the liars who are scorned. We have become so accustomed to being lied to, we call it by a high-sounding name, the credibility gap, as though the euphemism makes the lie somehow more acceptable. Liars and the lied-to are accomplices.

The alienation so rampant today is primarily the anxiety of a people who no longer know what the bounds are, who can no longer distinguish truth and falsehood and whose serenity comes through the denial of the paradoxes and contradictions inherent in American society. Two problems are foremost: the problem of money, and how to get it; the problem of color, and how to exalt it.

We all know that our stated ideals—the four freedoms, the Bill of Rights, the Constitution and the Declaration of Independence—have never seriously stood in the country's way of making a buck or mistreating a black. These perpetual lapses compromised, when they did not sacrifice, the moral integrity of American society. The problem with America is not that it is in some vague way sick, but that in many specific ways it is corrupt. And the origin of that corruption may be found in the self-delusion of racism and the immorality of capitalism.

It is racism that dismisses the humanity of the world's colored population. It is racism that disdains the peoples of Asia and Africa and South America as "niggers abroad." It is racism spawned within America's borders that now colors her world-view. It divides the earth into those who rule and those who serve. It determines whether a man's lineage is acceptable or not, just as it decides when people shall eat (Kansas), and when they shall not (India). It decides what government will be supported (Bolivia), and which shall be cut down (Vietnam). Racism decides what countries shall be invaded (the Dominican Republic), and which shall not (South Africa). In truth, racism does not make America freedom's foremost advocate, but its foremost danger.

But blacks have always known this. "The Negro," James Baldwin says, "has the great advantage of having never believed that collection of myths to which white Americans cling: that their ancestors were all freedom-loving heroes, that they were born in the greatest country the world has ever seen, or that Americans are invincible in battle and wise in peace, that Americans have always dealt honorably with Mexicans and Indians and all other neighbors or inferiors, that American men are the world's most direct and virile, that American women are pure. Negroes know far more about white America than that."

Of course, black vision, like black lives, has never really counted. Until now. Now, all the things blacks ever said about America, things white America rejected as unthinkable, have come to pass. John Kennedy and Martin Luther King and Robert Kennedy are dead. But they were simply the most radiant and most eminent of the victims.

The problem is not only race, though that is its biggest part. It is the society itself, kids freaking out, water polluted, air unfit to breathe. Yet, none of these things are thought to be indicative of the corruption in the state. They are (they say) temporary aberrations. Bodies tumble in the street and the litany grows louder: "America is always right . . . America is the aggrieved party. . . . The fault lies not in our society but in our critics. They are mad. Insanely, jealously mad. . . ." For a moment we are anxious, but it passes. The defenders of the faith spring into action and the American gospel lulls us back to sleep.

When it comes time for a reckoning, we must not forget these hucksters. The sharp-eyed boys whose fortune is tied to the preservation of the mythology. China, they told us, is all that's behind Hanoi; and Hanoi is all that's behind the National Liberation Front. Books were written, training films made, to propagate these tales, rationales for murder. Now, it is clear that nothing of the kind is the case. But no one says, We have been lied to.

In the midst of this contamination, the black struggle rages for Victory. That it should be a black struggle has been predetermined by its adversary, which is white power. James Boggs, black writer from Detroit, has described it best:

> Is it white power which decides whether to shoot to kill (as in Watts) or not to shoot at all (as in Oxford, Mississippi, against white mobs); to arrest or not to arrest, to break up picket lines or not to break up picket lines, to investigate brutality and murder or to allow these to go uninvestigated; to decide who eats and who goes on city aid when out of work and who does not eat and does not go on city aid; to decide who goes to what schools and who does not go; who has transportation and who doesn't; what streets are lighted and have good sidewalks and what streets have neither lights nor sidewalks; what neighborhoods are torn down for urban renewal and who and what are to go back into these neighborhoods. It is white power which decides what people are drafted into the army to fight and which countries this army is to fight at what moment. It is white power which has brought the United States to the point where it is counterrevolutionary to, and in-

creasingly despised by, the majority of the world's people.[1]

Some Historical Notes

Both the culture of racism and the drive to empire are as old as the nation. In 1783 George Washington described America as a "rising empire." William Henry Drayton, Chief Justice of South Carolina during the Revolution, was more glowing:

> . . . thus has suddenly arisen in the world, a new empire, styled the United States of America. An empire that as soon as started into existence attracts the attention of the rest of the universe; and bids fair, by the blessing of God, to be the most glorious of any upon record.[2]

Drayton's prophecy was fulfilled: America marched into the sunlight of world civilization—never mind that it was over broken bodies—to the present age of unraveling myths, freedom, justice and equality.

African slaves were the cornerstone of the developing national economy not only with respect to the South's plantation system, but also in the shipping and distilling industries of the North. Indeed, Britain's triangular trade from Liverpool to Africa to the West Indies was forced to compete with the Boston to Africa to South Carolina triangle of rum, sugar and slaves.

At the dawn of the American Revolution, it seemed that the nation might transcend its nearly two-hundred-year investment in slavery. James Otis, in *The Rights of the British Colonies,* wrote of the Negro's "inalienable right to freedom." Jefferson, in *A Summary View of the Rights of British America,* said abolition was "the greatest object of desire in the colonies" and accused Britain "of consistently blocking all efforts to end the slave trade." He also included a specific condemnation of slavery in his draft of the Declaration of Independence:

> . . . He (King George) has waged cruel war against human nature, violating its most sacred rights of life and liberty in the persons of a distant people who never offended him, captivating and carrying them into slavery in another hemisphere, or to incur miserable death in their transportation thither. The piratical warfare, the opprobrium of infidel powers, is the warfare of the Christian king of Great Britain. Determined to keep open a market where man should be bought and sold, he has prostituted his negative for suppressing every legislative attempt to prohibit or to restrain this execrable commerce. . . .

The passage was deleted, however, and later Jefferson explained why:

> The clause reprobating the enslaving of the inhabitants of Africa was struck out in complaisance to South Carolina and Georgia who had *never* attempted to restrain the importation of slaves and who, on the contrary, *still wished to continue it.* Our Northern brethren also I believe felt a little tender under those censures for though their people had very few slaves themselves *yet they had been pretty considerable carriers of them to others.*[3]

The slave trade laid at King George's feet was freely engaged in by the colonists, and freely continued. The colonial "revulsion" against King George's practice of slavery evaporated before its own interests. The double standard of racism corrupted America; its doctrines and institutions were, and are, subordinated to racial expediency. To keep black men in slavery the nation betrayed its legal system; to prevent slave insurrections it established an arbitrary police power; to ease its conscience it formulated a mythology of racial superiority. True liberty cannot come to America until American myths are rejected, until America faces the fact that its institutions commit social inequities rather than correct them; that its laws and religions and governments oppress black peoples within the country and without. For America, both nation and empire, is the principal overlord of the world.

> Afro-American slavery, the decimation of the indigenous Indian population, their deprivation and confinement in concentration-camp reservations; the military conquest of a large part of the national territory of the Mexican people and their dispossession from ownership of the land, the overthrow of Reconstruction's noble effort at representative government and the nullification of the Constitutional amendments, the establishment of the state system of racial segregation (enforced by the police-power and the lynch mob), the systematic cultivation of white racial-supremacy theories of government by the leading educational institutions of the nation and the application of these theories in the wholesale disfranchisement of the black population in the Southern states, as well as in the conquest of the Philippines, Puerto Rico and Guam . . . was the main path by which America ascended to the position of world power by the turn of the 20th century.[4]

American world power, so omnivorously acquired and stoutly defended, unites men throughout the world against it. They seek a revolution almost literary in nature which arises out of their desire to define themselves in a world where they have always been defined by others.

The shame of the times is that this revolution veers unerringly to blood. The inexorable confrontation lies in the refusal of the privileged to relinquish their power, and the recognition of the victimized that without power they are lost. As Han Suyin has noted, the consciousness of the oppressed is an unwitting gift from their oppressors.

> . . . if today China is Communist, it is the Western powers which forced her into it, and if the peoples of Asia are beginning to believe that nothing can be achieved except by the power of the gun, it is because this was proved by decades of violence. Everyone is conditioned by experience, our future made before we are born. Today the same lesson is being taught to future generations, the lesson that the gun is the sole arbiter in the end and it is still the West which teaches the lesson.[5]

When this perception is shared by America's victims, there will be an end to mythology, and an end to confusion. It will be the time of the harvest. And America will take its place in history—by the side of Rome.

Postscript

Some will say that this indictment is too broad, that not all whites are either racist or evil. That is so, but that is not the issue. What is at issue is the basic nature of American society and the relation of white Americans to that society. One knows that not all whites have been involved in the specific acts of oppression. But all whites, in varying ways, benefit from that oppression. And most suffer it in silence.

We do concede that there are good white men in America, but where does that leave us? Undoubtedly there were good Germans too, but the Jew-killers were not stopped there and the nigger-killers have not been stopped here. Nor was the Nazi rape of Europe averted, or the American rape of Africa. So, when we have made that admission, what exactly will have changed?

Indeed, the things that unite America with Germany may be more than those that divide them. There is really nothing to choose between "America, right or wrong" and "Deutschland über Alles." For, when chauvinism supplants reason, all crimes are permissible. And what was unspeakable yesterday is commonplace today.

It will be well, at that time, not to mistake America's false glitter for real light. We should, instead, mourn its lost and faded dream. And, maybe, in the bright glare that comes before the darkness, we might bid the country Robinson Jeffers's ultimate salute: "Shine, Perishing Republic."

> While this America settles in the mould of its vulgarity,
> heavily thickening to empire,
> And protest, only a bubble in the molten mass, pops
> and sighs out, and the mass hardens,
>
> I sadly smiling remember that the flower fades to make
> fruit, the fruit rots to make earth.
> Out of the mother; and through the spring exultances,
> ripeness and decadence; and home to the mother.

NOTES

1. James Boggs, *The City Is the Black Man's Land,* p. 8.
2. Richard W. Van Alstyne, *The Rising American Empire* (Quadrangle Books, 1965), p. 1.
3. St. Clair Drake, *The American Dream and the Negro,* The Emancipation Proclamation Lectures, Roosevelt University, 1963, p. 13.
4. *Ibid,* p. 14.
5. J. H. O'Dell, "Foundations of Racism in American Life," *Freedomways,* Vol. IV, No. 4, 1964, p. 515.

INTERNATIONAL LAW IN A REVOLUTIONARY WORLD

Frans A. M. Alting von Geusau

In the world around us, a revolutionary process of rapid social change is shaping the society we live in—"We now find ourselves in a period of transition from the ontological to the functional periods of human history."[1] Urban societies are replacing rural or small-town communities; the search for safety in closed religious communities is disappearing because of the desire to be functionally inspired in open churches cooperating mutually. States are no longer those "perfect" political communities once considered to be sufficient in themselves for promoting the well-being of their inhabitants. In our present society of technology, the jet plane, the nuclear revolution and decolonization, man has to choose between well-being, as a fruit of global cooperation, and destruction, poverty or violation of human rights, as a consequence of persistent international anarchy.

It must be said, with the late Pope John XXIII, "that at this historical moment the present system of organization and the way its principle of authority operates on a world basis no longer correspond to the objective requirements of the universal common good."[2] It is here that one of the crucial problems of our present age is to be found. Man now lives in the tension between a revolutionary process of change and an outmoded traditional organization of society which is incapable of coping with it. The process is marked by an increasing interdependence of peoples, although the international system is still founded on the independence of sovereign nation-states. The existence of nuclear weapons requires collective security on a global level, but the nation-states still cling to regional or separate arrangements for self-defense.

The welfare of mankind can be achieved only through worldwide economic cooperation and global economic policies; the system at present is still based on competition between national or block economic policies. "Everyone is entitled to a social and international order in which the rights and freedoms set forth" in the Universal Declaration of Human Rights "can be fully realized;"[3] the persistence of international disorder results in the constant violation of these rights and freedoms. Man now is a citizen of a world society in which everybody has become his neighbor; legally and mentally he still is a national citizen, whose loyalties are exclusively directed toward his own separate state. Peaceful cooperation and peaceful change have become the only reasonable instruments for promoting world order and individual well-being; but war and violence continue to be used as instruments for dealing with international conflicts.

The present international situation clearly manifests the

tragedy of these profound tensions. We are advocating change but accept it only at the expense of our neighbor or adversary. We condemn nuclear war, but we continue the arms race. We talk about the need to strengthen the authority of the United Nations as an indispensable condition for gradual disarmament; at the same time, we keep the organization weak in the very exercise of its peace-keeping mission. Impressive documents such as *The United Nations Development Decade*[4] are being written; before five years of the decade were over, however, it became clear that even the modest goal set forth in this document proved to be too ambitious, while at the same time the gap between rich and poor nations continued to widen, defense spending continued to increase, and development assistance remained marginal and unorganized.

More disturbing still is the present international situation, if we consider the policies of some major states individually. In Vietnam a cruel and inhuman war is being fought, dominated by consideration and analysis of the power politics involved, and with "much less concern for the tremendous human suffering which the conflict has entailed for the people of Vietnam and also for the people of other countries involved in the fighting".[5] Soviet military intervention in the internal affairs of Czechoslovakia in 1968 again violated the rights and aspirations of a whole nation. Dominated as this invasion was by a dangerously anachronistic conception of power politics, it crushed the hopes and yearnings of those striving for détente, peace and security on the European continent. Notwithstanding the tragic economic situation in their countries, India and Pakistan fought in 1965, wasting their energies and resources in a conflict they have so far been unable to solve peacefully. In the Middle East, states once more resorted to war in 1967 over a conflict they are unwilling to solve. As a consequence, the prospects for peace in that area appear to be more remote than ever before. White supremacy in the southern part of Africa is inevitably leading to a major international conflagration without any prospect or even willingness for change. In Western Europe, finally, the continent which has brought untold sorrow to mankind, the postwar era of hope and effort to build new international structures is over. Statesmen again work for independence, status and prestige, more concerned as they are about their own role in power politics than about their contribution to world peace. Hardly more than twenty years after the Second World War, our states, faced with the possibility of total destruction, have returned to the normalcy of the old devices of anarchy, power politics, self-interest and minor diplomatic maneuvering.

If this is the shape and style of modern international society, we may well ask ourselves what function law can perform to promote world peace. In the context of the present world situation, it should be quite clear that the lawyer can perform this function only if he is willing and able "to extend [his] aspirations beyond the traditional exercises in technical formulae for determining what conduct is lawful and what unlawful to the much more urgent task of determining and recommending that international law which is best designed to promote a free world society."[6] He will also have to dissociate himself from the traditional theory which conceives of international law as a separate body "of customary and treaty rules which are considered legally binding by States in their intercourse with each other,"[7] leaving the lawyer no other task than to study the conduct of governments and suggest minor technical improvements.

He should, instead, become the creative lawyer who develops a system of law—of which international law is a basic component—which may become a body of principles, standards and rules to protect human dignity and to promote the development of the human personality and the creation of world order. In doing so, he would help to give international law a vital function in decreasing the distance between the subsisting structure and the revolutionary process of social change, with a view to adapting the structures to the need of guiding the process of change.

Assuming that the existing international organizations are the best available instruments for gradually transforming the present interstate system into a new and more functional one, the lawyer should focus his attention on transforming these organizations into the major agencies for promoting such a new law and a new structure in international relations.

Keeping this basic assumption in mind, we will examine the present state of legal theory and international practice and the possibilities of developing a new law that can be made a better instrument for promoting social change and world peace.

LEGAL THEORY: THE PITFALLS OF THE TRADITIONAL COMPARATIVE APPROACH

If we compare our national societies with the present international system, the unavoidable conclusion is that the latter's fundamental problem consists in the absence of authoritative legal and political institutions having the power to ascertain the law, to promulgate new law and to enforce the law in force. Hence the conclusion drawn by many lawyers that only the formation of a world government can ultimately cure the disease of international anarchy. Having drawn such a conclusion, some lawyers then set themselves to work out yet another scheme for a federal type of world state, while others, disregarding the so-called unrealistic world federalists, return to their description of traditional state practice in foreign relations.

Both schools of thought, however, share two basic errors. First of all, their theories conceive the historic phenomenon we call a state as being the exclusive device for organizing political life. In their state-centered approach, society can only evolve from a world of states to a world of one state. Their conception of world order is furthermore a static one. Rather than focusing on functions to be performed by whatever means appropriate in a dynamic world society, they turn their attention to proposing governmental institutions resembling traditional structures of the existing states.[8] Their theories neglect both the depth of the social change that is now taking place and the fundamentally dialectic character of the process itself.

As a consequence, their schemes propose the formation of larger statelike territorial units, for which they use the traditional federal state as their model. According to this model, the federal state is a superstructure over preexisting states, taking over such powers as are necessary for acting as a unit in international relations. The component states preserve their autonomy in other fields. The actual delimitation of powers between federation and states in each historic case depends on a number of political and geographical circumstances. A large measure of consensus, however, appears to exist on the necessity of including at least defense, foreign affairs and a number of economic and financial matters in the powers conferred upon the new superstructure. The federal state also stands as model for the institutional provisions proposed in those schemes. They normally include an executive council, a legislative body in which various balances are provided for representation of the component units and popular representation, a judiciary and various more specialized authorities.

Examples of two such schemes may now be discussed briefly.

The first is the scheme once proposed for a Western European federation or political community.[9] The proposed community was to have a number of missions and aims in the fields of foreign policy, defense and economic affairs. Within these fields its powers were restricted to those already conferred upon the European Coal and Steel Community (ECSC) and the proposed European Defense Community (EDC), to the coordination of the foreign policies of member states and to the progressive establishment of a common market. Institutionally, the community was to have an executive council, a council of national ministers, a parliament composed of a people's chamber and a senate representing the people of each state, a court and an economic and social council. The detailed provisions for the composition of the institutions and the decision-making procedures were in sharp contrast with the powers actually conferred upon them. This marked contrast brought Friedrich to the conclusion "that the Statute definitely is calculated to prevent that process of "federalizing" governmental activities which has been a characteristic of existing federations and has been a most helpful factor in their steady development and growth."[10] The basic shortcoming of the scheme, however, should not be sought in its institutional weaknesses but rather in its traditional and nonfunctional approach to the modern problem of European integration. In terms of functions to be performed by an integrating Europe in 1953—and still more today—traditional thinking made the drafters choose exactly the wrong ones. But the primary aim of integrating Europe has been to contribute to a better world order by a process of overcoming past divisions. In this sense, the pooling of basic industries (coal and steel) clearly met the "test of functional performance."[11] The choice of defense and foreign policy did not meet this test in the context of a little Europe. On the one hand, the coordination of foreign and defense policies was and is doomed to be the least successful effort to overcome past divisions. On the other hand, the concentration on those functions which might enable the possible new superstructure to act as a unit in international relations neglected the dialectic character of the process to attain more world order. History gives no proof for the argument that a smaller number of larger sovereign states can better promote world order than a larger number of smaller states. On the contrary, the more powerful a state is in an unorganized international society, the more inclined its leaders are to pursue their aims by force if deemed necessary.

The traditional approach to world order in a regional context thus points to two conclusions: (1) the application of the test for the new unit of "institutional resemblance" with preexisting federal states entails a marked disregard for "functional performance" both internally and in a world context; (2) the approach neglects the more fundamental problem of the present structure of international society, which is the existence of sovereign territorial states. The future of the world does not ask for a smaller number of those units but for a larger number of different and diversified units to act in international society.

The second example concerns one among various schemes for establishing a world government. Here, I shall briefly discuss the well-known proposals made by Clark and Sohn in their book *World Peace through World Law.*[12] Presented as a plan for a revised and strengthened United Nations organization, their scheme affords an interesting example of traditional legal thinking about world affairs. The new powers to be conferred upon the revised organization were to be restricted to matters directly related to the maintenance of peace—that is to say, the proposals embodied the three classical approaches to peace: peaceful settlement of disputes, a system of international security, and a procedure for gradual disarmament. Within the limits of these powers, the plan proposed a strengthening of existing UN institutions according to a model of the federal type. The new general assembly was to become the top organ of the organization, with as much legislative power as required for implementing the rules laid down in the revised charter. It was to be composed of representatives from member countries elected by national parliaments and later by universal suffrage. The security council was to become an executive council, subordinated to the authority of the general assembly, and directing the disarmament inspection agency, the world police force, the nuclear energy authority and the world space agency. Judicial authority was to be exercised by a strengthened international court of justice for legal disputes, and by a new world equity tribunal for nonlegal disputes. In addition, a world conciliation council was provided, as well as regional courts subordinated to the international court of justice.

World peace through world law affords a classic example of a static approach to world peace which appears to be inherent in the legalistic attitude toward solving world problems. Instead of attacking the problem at its roots—the existing state structure—it merely superimposes a new statelike structure, while otherwise preserving the traditional system, such as the states' right of self-defense, notwithstanding the obligation to disarm. The scheme also fails to propose adequate provisions—other than those already written in Article 14 of the UN Charter—for promoting processes of peaceful change. Should the world equity tribunal be proposed to serve such a purpose, we can only agree with Kunz who once wrote that such a "proposal starts from the mistaken idea that world history can be reduced entirely to court procedure."[13]

Most conspicuously, however, the plan has failed to test the potential functional performance of the scheme in the context of the present process of rapid social change. It concentrated on strengthening those powers which are least likely in the present era of change to be conferred by states upon a world authority. At the same time it neglected the functions to be performed in the fields of economic, social, humanitarian and technical affairs which are now most likely to create conditions for promoting a peaceful world (although a later proposal did add a world development authority).

The traditional approach to world order in a universal context—as exemplified by the Clark-Sohn scheme—thus points to conclusions similar to those drawn from the approach to world order in a regional context: (1) the disregard of functional performance as a result of seeking institutional resemblance and (2) the neglect of the necessity to break through a state-centered structure of society in favor of a problem-centered network of functional units operating on the most appropriate levels.

INTERNATIONAL PRACTICE: LAW AS AN INSTRUMENT TO PRESERVE THE STATUS QUO

State practice and the functioning of a number of important international organs provide striking examples of employing legal techniques for concealing the states' unwillingness to promote processes of peaceful change. This unwillingness can best be illustrated by discussing a number of significant cases in three areas where change appears to be extremely urgent.

Peaceful Settlement of Disputes over Territory

In the international system of independent, juxtaposed states, territorial possession delimits state jurisdiction and authority, the development of its population and the access to natural resources and axes of communication. Most existing frontiers or armistice lines have been drawn by force and by virtue of peace treaties and armistice agreements. Hence the importance of provisions in the Covenant of the League of Nations and the Charter of the

United Nations for making organized international society both guarantee the territorial integrity of states and provide for the possibility of changing unsatisfactory situations through peaceful procedures.

In the existing system, acceptable delimitations of frontiers are a vital condition for peaceful relations, whereas territorial-conflict situations easily degenerate into grave disputes endangering international peace. Territorial rights under international law are being based almost exclusively on the primitive rule of effective possession. Neither the law nor state practice has been able or willing so far to apply more creative and effective new rules for enabling the League or the UN to solve territorial disputes. When the League of Nations was being organized, Woodrow Wilson introduced the principle of self-determination of peoples and the criterion of the interests of the population for arranging interstate boundaries, rejecting the right to "hand peoples about from sovereignty to sovereignty as if they were property."[14] At the Versailles peace conference, the principle of national self-determination was applied with hardly any consistency. The criterion of the interests and well-being of peoples found its way into the Covenant only within the restricted framework of the mandate system. In the UN charter the principle of self-determination of peoples was accepted as basic in Article 1(2). The criterion of the interests of the population was included both in the declaration regarding non-self-governing territories and in the international trusteeship system. At the same time, an advisory role was given to the League Assembly and the UN General Assembly in dealing with necessary changes in territorial situations.[15]

The record of dealing with territorial disputes on the

basis of this principle and criterion has not been promising so far. The continuingly dangerous situations in countries and areas like Korea, Vietnam, Kashmir, Palestine, Central Europe, the Portuguese colonies and South-West Africa—to mention only the major ones—and along many existing frontiers, give proof of the inability of the UN and the unwillingness of the states concerned to solve their territorial disputes peacefully and on grounds other than actual possession. In only a few territories (the Saar mandates and trusteeship territories) which were placed under international supervision as a result of the two world wars could the formation of new and independent states be promoted by applying the principle of self-determination. In most other cases, where decolonization fostered the formation of new states, the process either resulted from the use of force or from political pressure as a consequence of the new balance of power in the postwar world. In many of these cases the maintenance of arbitrarily delimited boundaries is engendering new territorial disputes between the newly independent states. The unwillingness to approach territorial problems in a creative and dynamic way is perhaps best demonstrated by the recent judgment of the International Court of Justice in the South-West Africa case submitted to it by Ethiopia and Liberia. Seldom has the World Court been given such an opportunity to set a legal precedent which might significantly contribute to a more peaceful society. The Court could speak on an aspect of international law that had already manifested progressive development; it was virtually assured of overwhelming support in the UN and held the unprecedented confidence of the new states. Nevertheless, the Court in fact refused to judge on the true merits of the case. In so doing, it helped to maintain a territorial situation which had clearly become unacceptable legally as well as politically. Let us briefly consider the situation and the judgment of the Court.

Dealing with the proposed mandate system in 1919, a serious conflict of opinion developed at the Versailles Conference concerning South-West Africa and the other overseas possessions of Germany. "Wilson and Lloyd George supported . . . the proposal that they should not be annexed by the Allies which had conquered them, but administered as mandated territories under the supervision of the League. They were opposed . . . by South Africa, which considered it necessary to [its] future security to annex . . . German South-West Africa. [After hot debate a compromise was reached: South Africa agreed that the territory] "should be placed under mandate, while the Supreme Council [of the Conference] agreed to appoint South Africa as mandatory for German South-West Africa. . . ."[16] Although the administration of the mandate was to be supervised on the basis of the criterion of the well-being of the population, the margin between annexation and a supervised mandate was very thin indeed. According to Article 22 (5) of the Covenant and Article 2 of the later decision of the League's Council, "the Mandatory shall have *full power of administration and legislation* over the territory subject to the present Mandate *as an integral portion of the Union of South Africa. . . .*"[17] From the point of view of the progressive development of international law, the new UN trusteeship system marked a significant improvement over the mandate system for so-called C territories. The supervisory powers of the UN over *all* trust territories were strengthened. The basic objectives, by virtue of Article 76 of the Charter, were changed so as to include "progressive development towards self-government or independence as may be appropriate to the particular circumstances of each territory and its peoples and the freely expressed wishes of the peoples concerned [and the encouragement of] "respect for human rights and for fundamental freedoms for all without distinction as to race. . . ."

UN members holding territories under mandate in 1945 were invited to place them under the trusteeship system. South Africa, however, used the argument of the termination of the League as a pretext for carrying out its original objective of annexing South-West Africa. It refused both to place the territory under trusteeship and to allow the UN organs to take over the original powers once exercised by the League.

The situation thus created—and unchanged so far—is perfectly clear: South Africa has returned to the pre-1914 legal conception of territorial rights, whereas the great majority in the UN General Assembly wishes it to accept the newly developed law as written in the UN Charter and further developed in the practices of the UN.

Faced with this unique situation, the Court has manifested an increasing unwillingness to perceive its role as an instrument for contributing toward the progressive development of international law. Basing itself on the permissive character of Article 77 of the Charter, the Court first took an intermediate position in its three advisory opinions on the South-West Africa case. On the one hand, it rejected South Africa's right to modify unilaterally the international status of the territory; on the other, it argued that the UN, the new law notwithstanding, could not exercise other functions or apply rules and standards other than those originally agreed upon in 1920 under the mandate.[18]

South Africa, however, proved to be unwilling even to accept this middle position pronounced by the Court. As a consequence, two UN members, having also been members of the League, decided to refer the case as a dispute to the Court. In doing so, they invoked Article 7 of the 1920 mandate agreement, which stipulates that "if any dispute whatever should arise between the Mandatory and another member of the League of Nations relating to the interpretation or the application of the provisions of the Mandate, such dispute, if it cannot be settled by negotiations, shall be submitted to the Permanent Court of International Justice. . . ." In 1962, the Court upheld the right of the two states to bring the dispute before it as well as its own jurisdiction to judge upon it, despite preliminary objections of South Africa. In 1966, adjudicating on the merits of the case, the Court in fact reversed its earlier judgment (although shaky legal arguments were employed to prove it was not reversing it). It rejected the claims of Ethiopia and Liberia, finding "that the Applicants cannot be considered to have established any legal right or interest appertaining to them in the subject-matter of the present claims."[19]

Leaving aside a further consideration[20] of more technical legal aspects and of the unequivocal language ("*another* member of the League") of the original 1920 agreement, the 1966 judgment manifests the inability or unwillingness of the Court to progressively develop that law which is best designed to promote world peace. Territorial disputes are the most difficult ones to solve, and if unsolved, the most dangerous ones for world peace.

Hence the importance of progressively developing the new law introduced by the League of Nations and the UN. This new law at least implies:

(a) that organized international society and the members of the UN have a legal right and interest in a territorial situation "the continuance of which is likely to endanger the maintenance of international peace";

(b) that this legal right and interest is all the more apparent in the case of a territory placed under the supervision of organized international society;

(c) that a dispute concerning the question whether South Africa is acting in accordance with the principle of self-determination and the criterion of the well-being of the population in South-West Africa may be submitted to the International Court of Justice.

The refusal of the Court to adjudicate in a case which was both politically relevant and accepted as being a legal dispute by all parties concerned, cannot but further exclude the World Court as an agency for developing international law. At the same time, it supports the practice of using law as an instrument for preserving the status quo in an area where a law promoting change is most urgently needed.

International Security in the Nuclear Age

On September 19, 1961 the U.S.S.R. and the United States issued a joint declaration recommending a number of principles as the basis for future multilateral negotiations on disarmament. One of these principles was that "progress in disarmament should be accompanied by measures to strengthen institutions for maintaining peace and the settlement of international disputes by peaceful means."[21] More specifically, the declaration referred to "the necessary measures to maintain international peace and security, including the obligation of states to place at the disposal of the United Nations agreed manpower necessary for an *international peace force. . . .*" In the 1960s the old truth of an indissoluble link between a progressively developing system of collective security and a gradual process of disarmament became more apparent than ever before. As the late President Kennedy said in his 1961 address to the UN General Assembly, the UN "will either grow to meet the challenges of our age—or it will be gone with the wind without influence, without force, without respect. Were we to let it die, to enfeeble its vigor, to cripple its powers, we would condemn our future. For in the development of this organization rests the only true alternative to war . . . Mankind must put an end to war—or war will put an end to mankind." Therefore, "the weapons of war must be abolished before they abolish us."[22]

In state practice, however, law is being used not as an instrument to develop the UN as the only true alternative to war but to keep it weak in order to retain national freedom of action. The states' inherent right of self-defense is being invoked to conclude alliances, to continue the arms race and to acquire nuclear weapons, instead of the inherent right of man to live in a peaceful, orderly world and to build and develop a system of collective security.

The so-called original intentions of the drafters of the Charter are being invoked to put an end to a new peace-keeping role that the United Nations was beginning to assume, instead of developing this role as being in conformity—in the sixties—with the UN purpose to maintain peace and security. The Secretary General is carefully being kept in his role as a "glorified" clerk, rather than being stimulated to act as the executive officer of the organization—a function also in conformity with the Charter.

The unwillingness to strengthen the United Nations as an alternative to war can perhaps be demonstrated best by briefly discussing the evolution of its peace-keeping role, and more specifically the attempts made to set up an international peace force.

In drafting the Charter of the United Nations, much emphasis was given to the need for strengthening the security system to avoid the impotence of the former League of Nations. The Charter indeed provides for enforcement action to be decided on by the Security Council, and for making armed forces available to the Council. The improvement over the League Covenant and the ensuing evolution of the League, however, is more apparent than real. The unanimity rule in the League Council did not find its place in the Charter, but was replaced by the unanimity rule for the big powers only (the so-called veto power of the permanent members of the Security Council). "Under the Charter the Security Council has power—which the League Council did not have, to take action against the small powers, but the experience of the past would seem to show that it is not the small powers, acting alone, who are most likely to disturb the peace . . . One is [thus] forced to the conclusion that so far as the actual possession of power is concerned, the United Nations has not advanced much beyond the League of Nations and that in comparable situations much the same result is to be anticipated."[23]

The evolution of the organization has shown the relative lack of improvement made in this respect. Negotiations on making troops available to the Security Council broke down in 1947, when the Military Staff Committee and the Council proved unable to reach agreement on the general principles under which the Council was to make agreements (under Article 43 of the Charter) with member states.[24] As a result of U.S. action in the Korean War (and Soviet absence in the Security Council) military assistance was indeed furnished by some forty states to the Republic of South Korea on recommendation of the Security Council. All efforts made since 1950 and through the Uniting for Peace resolution to "codify" this Korean practice have failed. After three years of fruitless deliberations in the Collective Measures Committee, which has the task of recommending measures for advance preparation for collective action, the General Assembly in fact put an end to these activities during its ninth session.[25]

A new development was set in motion, however, at the time of the 1956 Middle Eastern crisis. In order to secure and supervise the cessation of hostilities and the withdrawal of British, French and Israeli forces from Egyptian territory, the General Assembly requested the Secretary General to set up, with the consent of the nations concerned, an emergency international United Nations force.[26] Since that time, the Security Council, on two other occasions, has agreed to send a UN police force to the Congo and Cyprus as a means of assisting the governments concerned in maintaining internal security. Comparable activities have been and are being carried out by large peace-observation missions in areas like Lebanon (1958), West Irian (1962), Yemen (1962–1964) and Kashmir (1949–1965). This new development, resulting from a new balance of power in the world and inside the UN, has two interesting characteristics.

First, instead of sending military forces with the aim of carrying out enforcement action against one or more states, the UN now sends police forces to supervise and ensure the implementation of an agreement or truce reached through negotiation inside the UN and with the consent of the nations concerned.

Second, instead of relying upon the combined power of the big states as a means to repel aggression, the UN now seeks to keep these same powers out, as a means to prevent further deterioration of the situation. As a consequence the Secretary General with his advisers, rather than the Security Council with its Military Staff Committee, has become the directing organ for peace-keeping operations. It is certainly clear that this evolution has been the most hopeful one in peace keeping since the UN came into existence. Reliance upon the police function of the UN rather than upon its military-enforcement function can widen the area of UN involvement without immediately requiring a force that is superior to existing national forces. It can do away with the traditional misconception that great powers that can win a war can also keep the peace, without, however, excluding their political influence in the negotiating process. Conflicts can thus be better isolated and ultimately solved, provided the UN members do not lose their interest once the UN is in the area.

It is also clear that the present world situation—the balance of terror, the role of the non-aligned countries, etc.—affords new opportunities for improving the system and strengthening the role of the UN and its Secretary General, and thus also facilitating disarmament.

Far from taking advantage of this promising development in UN activities by developing and creating new legal rules for peace keeping, the member nations have allowed the organization to fall into a new series of serious political crises: crisis over the financing of UN peace-keeping operations and crisis over the role of the UN Secretary General. Although the total costs of UN peace-keeping operations represent less than 0.3 percent of the amounts spent for national defense, member states have so far been unable to solve the crisis because of their collective unwillingness to make the UN into the instrument the world needs today. They simply ignore the serious consequences resulting from their "lack of new ideas and fresh initiatives and a weakening of the will to find means of strengthening and expanding genuine international co-operation." This means that "in respect of one of its most important activities, that of peace keeping, the promise held out by the demonstrated usefulness and success of our extensive operations in recent years has remained unfulfilled because of the continuing failure to agree on basic principles."[27]

(The hopeful developments in UN involvement were seriously jeopardized by the Middle East crisis of May–June 1967. When tension again increased dangerously between Israel and Egypt, President Nasser requested the withdrawal of the UN police force, which might have contributed to the prevention of a new war. In the UN itself, no effort was made to maintain the police force. After the Middle East war, again no attempt was made to revive the idea of a force for supervising the armistice. Instead, the major powers, and especially the U.S.S.R., concentrated on rearming their "clients" in this explosive area. As a consequence, the UN has so far been unable to exert any meaningful influence on the events in the Middle East. Its incapacity and the unwillingness of its members to make the organization an effective framework for peace keeping may well have brought an end to a development by which peace could have been promoted.)

States invoking the law of the Charter apparently do so, not as a means to further develop the organization, but as a pretext for returning to a pre-nuclear freedom of action.

Disarmament and the United Nations

If peace is to be promoted through the efforts of the United Nations, peaceful settlement of disputes (mostly territorial) and the building of a system of international security should be accompanied by measures for gradual disarmament. The close link between these "approaches to peace"[28] was already formulated in the League of Nations Covenant and in the UN Charter. According to the Charter (Articles 11 and 26) the responsibility for regulating armaments was to be shared by the General Assembly (formulating principles) and the Security Council (establishing the system). The story of disarmament negotiations[29]—except one brief chapter in the Kennedy era in which the first concrete measures of arms control were agreed upon—is among the most distressing annals in UN history. Two examples may suffice here to underline the tragedy of this long story.

Since the establishment of the Atomic Energy Commission in January 1946 by the UN General Assembly, efforts have been made to eliminate and prohibit nuclear weapons, the possession of which is certain to endanger international peace. Since 1946, however, the weapon has been developed far beyond its capacity to destroy human life on earth; its possession has spread from the United States to four other states (the U.S.S.R., Great Britain, France and China), and many other states are now capable of acquiring it. Notwithstanding the extreme danger of this situation and massive support for General Assembly resolutions against proliferation, the outdated and dangerous motives for so-called individual (state) security, prestige and status are still rated higher than the objective of creating a world society in which it is safe for humanity to live. As a consequence, the nuclear powers continue to develop their weapons and continue to reject the conclusion of significant additional agreements on arms control, while some potential nuclear powers remain unwilling to abandon their option of going nuclear.[30]

Although a treaty on the nonproliferation of nuclear weapons was signed and accepted in 1968 by an overwhelming majority in the UN General Assembly, it still needs ratification by most of the signatory states before it can take effect. The Soviet invasion of Czechoslovakia lessened the prospects of general ratification at an early date.

One of the equally disturbing facts—in the light of the many schemes for reducing armaments since 1947—has been the recent increase in the sale of conventional armaments to "countries outside the direct East-West confrontation and in *areas where active or potential local conflicts exist.*"[31] (Italics are mine.) What is disturbing here is not so much the understandable eagerness of new states in a peaceless world to accept foreign weapons, but the ambiguous policy of the major Eastern and Western powers.

In the inter-war years the manufacture and distribution of armaments were mainly in private hands. The "grave objections" against such activities in Article 8 of the League's Covenant resulted in regular information about the sale of armaments. During the Second World War, the freedom of private arms manufacturers largely disappeared.[32] Grave objections that are now raised against the distribution of armaments by governments were not written into the UN Charter. As a consequence, arms distribution flourishes unchecked and unpublicized. How hypocritical governmental policies can be in this area can be shown by the contradictory moves of the United States and Britain (who set examples followed by many other governments). The two governments recently created high-level bodies for dealing with disarmament: the Arms Control and Disarmament Agency in the U.S. administration and the Minister of State for Disarmament in Britain. Both governments, however, also created (more recently) the office of an international arms salesman, whose task is to promote the sale of armaments to other countries.[33]

Is it any wonder that the arms trade, promoted by the governments themselves, resulted, for instance, in the failure of the UN weapons embargo on the Republic of South Africa, and in the continuation of the fighting between Nigeria and Biafra?

International Practice: Some Conclusions

Our discussion has been focused on the three crucial approaches to peace embodied in the UN Charter: peaceful settlement of territorial disputes, international security and disarmament. Throughout the discussion, we have assumed[34] that the application of the Charter in our age of rapid social change allowed for a dynamic interpretation and evolution of its principles, standards and rules, because it is based on the overriding necessity for peace in a nuclear era. Our conclusion now must be that state practice has abused the law of the Charter in order to preserve the status quo. The limited acceptance of the International Court of Justice as the principal agency for determining and developing the law can only become even more so, as a result of the Court's own unwillingness to meet its responsibilities.

This brings us back to the fundamental crisis in international law and society, and to the law's fundamental task of creating conditions for a peaceful world and thus changing the structure of international society.

A NEW LAW TO PROMOTE SOCIAL CHANGE?

A new law designed to promote world peace requires the elaboration of that law that can be an instrument of international integration. Law may become such an instrument if three basic assumptions are accepted as starting points for changing legal theory and state practice: (1) that the international integration process is inherently dialectic in character, requiring the evolution toward different structures rather than larger similar structures in society; (2) that there is need for exploring other more functional approaches to peace through which conditions may be created for better enabling humanity to foster peaceful change; and (3) that the present crisis basically is a moral and spiritual crisis of a society which has diverted our loyalties from the human person and his well-being—as a creature of God—to man-made political and social systems.

The Dialectic Character of the Integration Process

In various works, Haas has defined international integration as "the process whereby political actors in several distinct national settings are persuaded to shift their loyalties, expectations, and political activities towards a new and larger center, whose institutions possess or demand jurisdiction over the pre-existing national states."[35] He called integration, defined in the context of a uniting Europe, the process of attaining political community as the terminal condition among the six member states of ECSC.

The foregoing analysis tried to show that we are less inclined to accept political community on a universal or regional level as a valid terminal condition. We are more interested in promoting cooperation by whatever means and on whatever level that may be appropriate for attaining world peace. We thus conceive of international integration as the process whereby *citizens* and political actors are persuaded to split their loyalties, expectations and political activities over several new and larger centers besides their own states, with a view to distributing and balancing jurisdiction among institutions designed for maximizing functional performance.[36]

This definition implies that a process of international integration should contribute to the attainment of a new condition in two respects: (1) on the one hand, the citizen—including the political actor—should change his political attitude to conform with the pluralistic society in which he now lives; (2) on the other hand, the present state-centered structure of society should be changed with a view to giving different associations and institutions, besides the existing states, the capacity to act in international society, and states be reduced to units performing useful functions besides those other bodies.

Citizenship today is currently being defined as the "quality requisite for the exercise of local political rights"[37] within a given state. Historically the process of abolishing privileges among citizens is closely linked with the rise of the nation-state. The nation-state, however, also replaced the multiplicity of ties (existing in the European Middle Ages) by the *exclusive* bond of national citizenship. The nationalization of citizenship thus promoted equality of rights within a given state; it contributed at the same time to the creation of new unequal privileges—with differences between national citizens and foreigners, and between the citizens of so-called Christian or civilized states and citizens of so-called non-Christian and less-developed countries. The psychological impact of nationalizing citizenship is still greater than its legal impact. The exclusive bond of national citizenship fostered the exclusive loyalty toward man's own political system, and active hostility, in certain situations, against the life and the existence of other peoples. It turned private wars into conflicts of nations, and reduced the citizen to no more than a pawn in the diplomatic chess game. It made the citizen accept the hatred that was built up against other peoples, and the notion that the preservation of his own political system has higher value than the well-being of human beings outside it.

Citizenship in a new world is therefore not just a matter of making national citizens into world-state citizens. It requires a fundamental change in our very concept of citizenship. The integration process in terms of the formation of citizenship is dialectic in character. National citizenship is not to be considered a milestone on the road to world citizenship; it is, in fact, the major barrier for teaching man to live in this changing world. The first task of citizen formation must therefore be to denationalize man's thinking, without attempting, however, to direct his exclusive loyalty to yet another and larger—for example,

European—territorially organized group or community. Man should be taught instead to refrain from giving exclusive loyalty to any political group and to live with a plurality of loyalties. A modern citizen may contribute to an improved world order if he is willing and capable, by splitting his loyalties, to prevent any state or any new center of power from using his exclusive loyalty for pursuing parochial ends. Law can perform a vital function by redefining citizenship along these lines and by suggesting new rules for organizing political participation according to the new concept.

New rules for political participation require the development toward a new poly-centered rather than state-centered international structure. In this respect, the integration process is equally dialectic in character. The well-known theory which views world history as an evolution toward ever-larger state-like structures (from tribes to one world state) is historically unfounded. The theory itself is a product of the nineteenth and twentieth centuries' idolization of the phenomenon called the state. The modern nation-state did not emerge out of an amalgamation of feudal or corporate societies; it emerged only when the preexisting social structure was destroyed. At the same time the emerging nation-states in Europe definitely broke down the relative cohesion once preserved by the pope and the emperor in the Middle Ages. The Renaissance princes were certainly justified in liberating themselves from papal domination over political affairs, but the process of transferring religious respect from the ecumenical church to the emerging secular states also created new and far more dangerous divisions in international society.[38]

Our modern global society is faced with comparable

problems in this period of transition, although our situation is new as a consequence of modern technology and the advent of the nuclear weapon. The problems are comparable because of the fact that the only way to create a peaceful world society is to abolish the existing state structure. In breaking down this structure, we should protect man against the form of technocracy in which he is going to lose essential rights of political participation acquired in his own national state. The situation is new to the extent that the transformation of the present structure cannot be achieved by force or violence. The necessary process of change can only evolve peacefully and thus gradually. The existing international organizations are the best available instruments for promoting such change.

It should be the function of the law to recommend new principles and rules for making them into instruments more effective than they are today. To that end, the lawyer should, first of all, change his basic conception of international law. Instead of conceiving it as a separate body of rules for regulating intercourse among states, he must learn to see international law as an integral part of the "common law of mankind,"[39] designed for promoting a peaceful world society. Under such a law, the human individual alone—and no longer the state—will possess the totality of rights and duties, nationally as well as internationally. The rights and duties of legal persons, including those of states under international law, must depend solely upon their purpose and functions.

A first objective of this law would be to elaborate principles and rules for promoting the well-being and personal development of man. Hence the necessity for recommending appropriate law-making processes and agencies within each functional context. This context may be a state, but must increasingly be some international organization or a nongovernmental body.

A second objective of the law would be to formulate rules for protecting man against the abuse of power by agencies set up to serve him. In our present society, states should be held primarily responsible for abusing their power and violating essential human rights. Hence the necessity for recommending—again within specific functional contexts—suitable methods for supervising the conduct of states, for doing justice to man and for enforcing such decisions.

A third objective of the new law should be to devise rules for assuring the citizen's participation in international decision making. In our existing democratic states, such participation is organized through various forms of representation; international society, in contrast, is inherently oligarchic in character, and governments only—and more often their foreign offices—can act on behalf of their states in international relations, and without being adequately controlled by national parliaments and citizens. Hence the necessity for recommending—within specific functional contexts—appropriate forms of participation and plural representation in the activities of all agencies concerned.

A final objective of the new law should be to recommend principles for gradually replacing the present balance of power between states by an institutionalized equilibrium of powers between several organs and agencies performing useful functions. Such equilibrium can emerge as soon as the citizen and the political actor are willing to shift part of their loyalty to new centers, whose institutions will acquire jurisdiction over the existing states in specific areas.

The lawyer can contribute to peace by elaborating on these objectives as soon as he forgoes the desire to draw up general schemes in favor of the much more urgent task of recommending that law which is best designed to foster change in specific functional contexts.

A More Functional Approach to Peace

Earlier in this essay we discussed the possibilities for approaching peace through peaceful settlement of disputes, building international security and promoting disarmament. Our conclusion was that states are as yet unwilling to promote peaceful change in these vital areas. The lawyer must therefore also focus his attention on developing new law in other areas where change can now be promoted, and through which better conditions may be created for making territorial possession and self-defense for states less important than they are today. "The main feature," wrote Jenks,[40] "of any long-range international policy must be the building up of a new body of international law relating to economic and social matters, the creation and effective application of which will make frontiers far less important than they are today."

Our functional approach to peace does not rest upon the dichotomy between political and nonpolitical problems with which international society has to deal. It tries to present rational means for promoting peaceful change and a change in the existing international structure.

Such a process cannot yet be set in motion in the vital areas already discussed. But it may be started in the equally vital field of economic and social cooperation, since poverty, hunger and disease can only be alleviated through world-wide cooperation, and also in such areas as meteorology and a world postal system. Peaceful change through functional cooperation also requires the creation of new institutions capable of exercising power over and beyond that of the existing states. This implies the necessity of strengthening and creating independent international institutions, and providing for plural representation of national interests. The latter may increase the possibilities for direct participation in international decision making and thus for depoliticizing the solution of international conflicts. Here again, the adoption of new law must be suggested for the performance of those functions in which states are willing to cooperate, and in which new institutions are capable of fostering a spill-over to other functions and (eventually) other states.

Finally, functional cooperation must deal with issues which are objects both of international and national policies. This implies that cooperation between a limited number of states may well affect adversely peaceful change on a world scale. It also implies that the prevailing heterogeneity of social, political and economic structures within the states severely limits the chances for assuring optimum functional performance among an optimum number of states—hence the necessity of choosing such areas in which the burgeoning cooperation between groups of states will not jeopardize the chances for extending cooperation to more states.

The more functional approach to world peace does not pretend to be a blueprint for world order or a comprehensive scheme for world peace. It tries to understand the change that is now taking place and to recommend measures for assuring that the process might be a peaceful and gradual one. It ultimately rests on the assumption that peace in the nuclear age is, as John F. Kennedy said,[41] "the most important topic on earth . . . as the necessary rational end of rational men" to be promoted by rational means.

Peace: The Most Important Rational End

In his address at Washington University, Kennedy said that when he spoke of peace he was "not referring to the absolute, infinite concepts of universal peace"; nor was he suggesting a "single, simple key to this peace . . . For peace is a process—a way of solving problems." Peace refers to an evolution in human institutions rather than a blueprint for a single world state. It refers to a way of changing present conditions, not to a terminal condition of human organization.

The lawyer, therefore, must focus on guiding the process as it develops rather than on formulating the product that might come tomorrow. This pragmatic approach to world order, Cox says, implies that man working at his "problems one at a time testifies to his belief in the order of things." He goes on to quote Morton:

> the fact that we approach life today without feeling the need for a big key that fits everything together as one great whole, and are able to concentrate instead on isolating particular issues and dealing with them as they come up, shows that we have a basic confidence that the world is held together, is strong, is self-consistent, has regularity in it and can be put to the test without everything in life going to pieces.[42]

This approach, which is adapted to the present society, should also inspire our approach to peace in international society.

The legal approach that this essay recommends does

not pretend to offer precepts for world order; it only suggests possibilities and opportunities for solving problems that must be solved if the world is to find peace. All these problems are ultimately man-made, and can be solved by human endeavor. Just as "wars begin in the minds of men, it is in the minds of men that the defences of peace must be constructed."[43] "The first and foremost moral precept that international society needs [is] that we learn to see human beings instead of groups or deterministic entities like the state, the economic system, development, progress etc."[44]

It is the urgent task of this generation to liberate humanity from its idolatry of the man-made state as the paramount expression of collective human power. If power is to be used for the common good, and not for total destruction, it has to be checked and balanced according to legal rules in a disorderly world. The lawyer has the means available for making law a creative instrument of peace.

NOTES

1. Harvey Cox, *The Secular City* (London, 1966), p. 64.
2. *Pacem in Terris* (encyclical).
3. Article 28 of the Universal Declaration of Human Rights.
4. Proposals for Action (New York: United Nations, 1962).
5. U Thant, Introduction to *The Annual Report of the Secretary General on the Work of the Organization, June 16, 1965–June 15, 1966,* General Assembly Official Records: Twenty-first Session, Supplement No. 1A (A/6301).
6. McDougal, "International Law, Power and Policy: A Contemporary Conception," *Recueil de Cours,* 1953, Vol. 82, p. 140.
7. Oppenheim and Lauterpacht, *International Law,* Vol. I (London, 1962), pp. 4, 5.
8. Compare Claude, *Swords into Plowshares: The Problems and Progress of International Organization* (New York, 1964), p. 393-94.

9. See especially Bowie and Friedrich, *Studies in Federalism* (Boston and Toronto, 1954).
10. *Ibid.*, pp. xli-xlii.
11. Claude, *op. cit.* p. 394.
12. Clark and Sohn, *World Peace through World Law* (Cambridge, Mass., 1960).
13. Kunz, "The Problem of Revision in International Law," *American Journal of International Law* (1939), Vol. 33, p. 50.
14. Snyder and Furniss, *American Foreign Policy* (New York, 1954), p. 31.
15. Article 19 of the Covenant and Article 14 of the Charter.
16. Walters, *A History of the League of Nations* (London, New York, Toronto, 1960), p. 58.
17. Italics are mine.
18. Exception made for the voting rules provided for in Article 18 of the UN Charter. The three advisory opinions are: international status of South-West Africa, ICJ Reports, 1951; voting procedure on questions relating to reports and petitions concerning the territory of South-West Africa, ICJ Reports, 1955; admissibility of hearings of petitioners by the committee on South-West Africa, ICJ Reports, 1956.
19. South-West Africa Cases, Second Phase, Judgment of 18 July 1966. ICJ Reports, 1966, p. 49.
20. See Higgins, "The International Court of Justice and South-West Africa: The Implications of the Judgment," *International Affairs*, Vol. 42, No. 4, October 1966.
21. Paragraph 7 of the Declaration.
22. *New York Times*, September 26, 1961.
23. Goodrich, "From League of Nations to United Nations," in Falk and Mendlovitz (eds.), *Strategy of World Order*, Vol. 3 (New York: United Nations, 1966), p. 24.
24. See especially Russell and Muther, *A History of the United Nations Charter* (Washington, D.C., 1958).
25. See the author's "Financing United Nations Peace Keeping Activities," *Netherlands International Law Review*, Vol. XII, No. 3, 1965.
26. *Loc. cit.*, p. 295. See also Wainhouse, *International Peace Observation* (Baltimore, 1966).
27. From U Thant's statement declining a second term as UN Secretary General, *New York Times*, September 2, 1966.
28. The term is used by Claude, *op. cit.*
29. See *Everyman's United Nations*, 7th ed., a basic history of the organization 1945 to 1953 (New York: United Nations), pp. 29-49.
30. See Buchan (ed.), *A World of Nuclear Powers?* (Englewood Cliffs, N.J., 1966).
31. Sutton and Kemp, *Arms to Developing Countries, 1945-1965*, Adelphi Papers No. 28 (Institute for Strategic Studies, October 1966), p. 1.
32. *Loc. cit.*, p. 4.

33. *Loc. cit.*, p. 1.
34. Cf. especially Claude, *op. cit.*, and Röling, *International Law in an Expanded World* (Amsterdam, 1960).
35. Haas, *The Uniting of Europe* (London, 1958), p. 6.
36. Italics mark the differences with Haas's definition.
37. Jessup, *A Modern Law of Nations* (New York, 1956), p. 73.
38. Compare Toynbee, *A Study of History* (London, New York, Toronto), Vol. I.
39. From Jenks, *The Common Law of Mankind* (London, 1958).
40. Jenks, "The I.L.O. and Peaceful Change," *New Commonwealth Quarterly*, Vol. IV, 1938–39, p. 367.
41. Speech, *New York Times*, June 11, 1963.
42. Cox, *op. cit.*, p. 66.
43. Preamble to the Constitution of UNESCO.
44. Landheer, *Ethical Values in International Decision-Making* (The Hague, 1960), p. 35.

EXCERPTS FROM A CORRESPONDENCE ON REVOLUTION AND LANGUAGE

Deirdre Levinson

I can't talk about the right and left wings any more. The right relies more heavily for its support on the psychological being, the left on the physical being. But the left is best because it contains the right in it, too. The left is, you know, rounded; it is the well-rounded left. The revolution marches, it is said, on its stomach. Emend from singular to plural: the revolution has two stomachs. The revolution is a fighting cow, its vital organs constituted of one stomach for the digestion of food, the other for the digestion of revenge. The great-spirited Wordsworth throws his lovely light on revenge in characterizing the Frenchman who sailed to Florida in 1568 to avenge the Spanish massacres of the French there:

> *Went single in his ministry across the ocean; not to comfort the oppressed, but, like a thirsty wind, to roam about withering the oppressor.*

That's a ministry that comes from the stomach. Once you understand that, there's no other ministry of comparable significance. The ministry of vengeance. The left-wing intelligentsia can't even identify the portfolio it carries. The army of the revolution has to identify it for them. This is perfectly demonstrated in a story by Isaac Babel about the ministry of the Red General Matthew Pavlichenko and how his landlord fared under it. "Then I stamped on my master, trampled him for an hour or maybe more. And in that time I got to know life through and through. With shooting—I'll put it this way—with shooting you only get rid of a chap. With shooting you'll never get at the soul, to where it is in a fellow and how it shows itself." An eye for an eye and a soul for a soul. The rebirth of the soul is effected by filling the two stomachs. The just distribution of the loaves and the fishes is no longer enough. You can't resurrect your soul on one stomach only. You can't have half a soul.

The idea of the "revolutionary" vision is that it is directed toward people and their agony. What other kind of revolutionary vision is there? The "masses" Rossellini has in mind, whose salvation lies in being brought back to beauty, are not the same masses as the two-thirds of the world's population who go hungry every day of their lives. Tolstoy answered the Rossellinis long ago: "We [the ruling class] in our relation to the poor man resemble the Old Man of the Sea. We will love and cherish him, we will preach the noblest morality to him, we will point out the beauties of the landscape and impart sweet music to him. We will do anything for the poor man—anything but get off his back." It isn't deprivation of beauty the masses suffer except in the real sense in which bread is beautiful to the breadless, or the plate of cheese to Brecht's peasant who encircles it with his arm and gazes at it sadly as he eats, because, "like all beautiful things, it is fast fading away."

Revolution in art and philosophy is indivisible from the political revolution; it is dependent on it, travels in its baggage train. It was only after the October Revolution that the Russians had their icons cleaned.

What I mean is, I don't know how to define. There's definition and definition, and the first definition's nothing once you know the second. For authoritative endorsement of which, see Edgar's speech concluding: "The wretch that thou hast blown unto the worst owes nothing to thy blast." Whereupon enter Gloucester with those two great black holes in his head, so that Edgar is forced to recant immediately, "I am worse than ere I was."

And that, as the Angelic Doctor said to the Manichees, settles your hash.

Nevertheless, I. A. Richards can define revolution. He lived in China before the Revolution and knows a war lord when he sees one. He was there too at the time of the Revolution when the war lords were made to bite the dust. Once I asked one of my old Oxford mentors—a person very extravagantly endowed by nature and fortune—what word she knew, really knew, to the bone. Underprivileged, she said. "In Rangoon we were excluded from the gymkhana-club." (She's one-eighth Burmese.) That was a very precise reply. Maybe someone will come up with the meaning of poverty—a rich man, no doubt.

So the revolutionary vision and its definition are inseparable from the people and their agony: it isn't a question of "directing" that vision toward the people. The people's agony is what the revolutionary agony is *about.* Socialism is about turning the poet's vision into action.

Socialism, Communism and Marxism seem to mean different things in the West. No serious Marxist would use these terms other than interchangeably. The haves and have-nots speak different languages, all but literally, and sometimes even that. Silone maintains somewhere that the peasantry of diverse countries understand each other's language better than the peasantry and bourgeoisie of the same country. But he may be stretching it a bit.

I'm currently writing a story which concerns a man on trial for treason against reality. He's permitted himself to be seduced from his absolute knowledge of the absolute reality of the eternity of nothingness by love and art—his mother and Giotto and Isaiah and all that lot. He's half dead as his trial begins, having been apprehended while attempting suicide in order to escape the intolerable truth; and he finally gives up the ghost in the course of the trial, which proceeds nonetheless. When it's all over, the dead man's attorney stands over him and says, "What's it like there?" The reply he gets is "No more words." Then, the attorney, as he walks home through the city, is struck by the terrible silence of all the people in the midst of their noise in the street, and recognizes that everyone has stopped talking aeons ago. (Everyone, that is, but the artists, the liars.) So he hails his fellows in the street, saying "How eloquent your silence is—this silence I am speaking of." I'm the attorney.

But the language of formulation is exclusively the possession of the haves, since they alone have access to education. The spokesmen for the have-nots, the rebel intelligentsia, are alone comprehensible to all sections of a class society, since while the protest they formulate is the property of the have-nots and eternally familiar to them, the expression of it is intelligible to the haves, and promptly utilized by them. Of all people the intelligentsia are the easiest and most rewarding to buy off, since their interests lie undeniably with the haves. The great weakness of a rising working class is that their leadership is drawn from the intelligentsia and that the intelligentsia always have one foot at least potentially in the enemy camp. The have-nots, when speaking among themselves, where the *condition* is taken for granted, use the word *poverty abstractly* about themselves. Marxist intellectuals never call the have-nots "the poor" and are not prone to dwell on their deficiencies, such as poverty. They regard that terminology as Christian with romantic overtones which they despise, regarding poverty, as they do, as a detestable and dishonorable condition, calling for—far from sympathy or pity—summary dispatch.

Revolution is a word reserved by the intelligentsia. Among those who identify with the bourgeoisie the word means change or development in any area of human thought or activity. Among those who have chosen to identify themselves with the exploited class, revolution specifies exclusively political change, the change of power from the hands of one class into the hands of the other. This change is unconstitutional and *invariably* violent, since what is meant today by change of power is the seizure by those who work the means of production and those who work the land of the means of production and the land.

Property for the owning class means capital investment either potentially or currently profitable. For the proletariat, property is only definable in negative terms: where they do use the word, it has no real reference. "Get off my property," they say to the invaders of their backyard (for which they pay rent to the real owner). It is a borrowed word in their vocabulary denoting something pretended to or about (as the Greeks called the raging Black Sea the Euxine, the Kindly One; or as the Jews at Auschwitz called, *inter alia,* the gas chambers Canada). The peasants' concept of property is identical with that of the large landowner, except that for them the meaning of property is not reserved to private property, since land held in common is a general feature of most peasant communities the world over. Insofar as private property has for them an equally real meaning, however, the peasantry, it is generally held, cannot be expected to form the leadership of a socialist revolution.

In the organization I belonged to in South Africa there were two men—an African leader known as the General and an Indian doctor called Goolam—who on one occasion went for a ride into the Cape countryside when the vineyards were in full fruit. Goolam, beholding them, would turn to his comrade and say, "General, how beautiful the vote is!" But they were intellectuals and ideas were their nourishment. No peasant could have said what Goolam said. I knew peasants who lived in town who dreamt of cattle and woke with awful nostalgia. There is a haiku: "Since there's no rice/Let us arrange/flowers in a bowl." I've seen it illustrated often enough among the have-nots, but not among the desperately poor. Beyond a certain point of acquaintance with agony, nothing is beautiful. When the Ancient Mariner saw the water snakes as beautiful, he simultaneously perceived the life in them and loved that life. But he'd only been in Hell for a week. The so-called Poor are called that by the haves with affectionate contempt. A time-worn euphemism for the vast group they have robbed with impunity for centuries, and to whose further degradation they contribute a fraction of their plunder as a solicited but unearned gift, known as charity. Jews have a blessing for practically everything but none for dispensing charity because—according to one rabbinical commentator (describing, all unaware, the Socialist form of the Incarnation)—God does not wish to have His name mentioned in so degrading an act. We should entreat the Church to shut up once and for all about the blessed meek inheriting the earth (six feet of it, if that), because the joke's gone bad on anyone who isn't too meek to keep the flies out of his eyes in central Africa. Only where the meek have succeeded in getting off their damn knees onto the barricades have they inherited the earth, and then the Church has been pensioned off summarily.

No man can act the part of a man without more than the bare necessities for physical survival, let alone less. There is therefore—as long as its opposite remains so inaccessible as to neutralize temptation—no more merit in the meekness of the have-nots than Malkin's maidenhead that no man desireth. Marx has amply demonstrated the reduced human capacity of the have-nots in all aspects, including their love for their own children. And yet—as one who can contemplate such niceties at leisure—I note a higher approximation to a common awareness of humanity among the have-nots than is notable among the dominant class. Which is not to say that poverty is a necessary ingredient for community. Still, common need as a common tradition can only advance the virtue of community up to a fixed point. In the concentration camps it was minimal, and yet it was there, too, in those in whom the techniques of humanity—ultimately inseparable from the techniques of physical survival—had been best fostered in normal life. The rich went first. Anyway, my own observation of the values and practices of the haves, their insensible and casual brutality, leads me to conclude that in the interests of surviving as a conscious human animal it is better to be an untouchable than advance in upward social mobility.

The only work proper to man, and the only work all men are capable of (given apt training), is thinking and the unremitting production of its fruits. This is the sole field offering sufficiently various and absorbing forms of specialized labor to enlarge the capacities of man and to counterbalance those of Satan. God was wrong in advocating gardening as the appropriate occupational therapy. But any work is better than none. See *One Day in the Life of Ivan Denisovitch.*

TWO

Definitions in Revolution

TIME AND REVOLUTION

Even such is time, which takes in trust
Our youth, our loves, our all we have,
And pays us but with age and dust—
Who in the dark and silent grave,
When we have wandered all our ways
Shuts up the story of our days . . .

This Sir Walter Raleigh is thought to have written the night before his execution, and it is the world's view of Time, active to seal up and to destroy, the picture of Chronos eating his children.

It is imaginative, but not true. There is no active malignity, no bitterness of hatred or warmth of affection, no wish to devour, in Time.

Himself inert, and in fact nonexistent, he is the sea in which men grow, are born, or die; and apart from his indifferent monotony, nothing in him is fixed to stand—no death, no splendor, no apotheosis, no end in sight—nothing but a neutral field for revolution.

In tapestries and allegorical pictures, nereids, tritons, seahorses, dolphins roll and play in a dark-blue ocean which has always appeared to me as the sea of Time. They emerge (usually halfway) and disappear, and it is unfair to blame the horizon-bounded playground for their disappearance. They have the sun and sky to watch them and the sea-rim for the arena of their world, and it is up to them not to mourn for the fact that the play time is limited, but to remember rather that for a short and brilliant interval the enlivening of that particular flatness of water rests in their hands alone. Their business, as I have just said, is revolution.

I like to contemplate revolution as something the tritons undertake for fun. It is surely a natural, but a mistaken, idea to think of it in more somber terms, a perversion of an everyday occurrence, much as if one were to consider eating in terms of indigestion only. To anyone who keeps his mind alive, revolution is easy as breathing, a briskness inherent in human nature, which, without it, would still be chipping flints (if indeed it had got so far). It is the mind's equivalent to the body's breathing, and Ideas fresh or faded should be as easy in their coming and their going as the physical air that empties and fills our lungs. It should, in fact, be a pleasant operation, and it is only because we have fallen into the habit of contemplating its grim side only that our attitude to revolution has come to be unfriendly.

There is a spring day when the fire feels too hot and doors are opened, and we decide to have our first meal out of doors: a small bustling takes place with tablecloths and glasses, and the life of the household is adapted to the spring. It is revolution in miniature, but it is genuine revolution—an adaptation to what is better for all concerned. If the housewife is recalcitrant, the thing becomes embittered and may fail; if the family chooses a bad day and the winter returns to pounce on them, the change will have to be given up and started again later; and if Granny suffers from bronchitis and cannot take the air, she will have to be wrapped in shawls or found a sheltered corner, or arranged in separate comfort altogether—for one cannot have revolutions, domestic or otherwise, that lop off from us human bits that are, after all, our own.

With these provisos, revolution is man's normal activity, and if he is wise, he will grade it slowly so that it may be almost imperceptible—otherwise he will jerk it in fits and starts and cause discomfort—but its game in either case will ever be that of the dolphins and tritons, emerging and disappearing in their sea of Time. And when he thinks it out, the revolutionary may be surprised to discover that the main necessity on both sides of a revolution is *kindness,* which makes possible the most astonishing things. To treat one's neighbor as oneself is still the fundamental maxim for revolutions.

Freya Stark

SILENCE

Silence is not merely an absence of noise. Real silence begins when a reasonable being withdraws from the noise in order to find peace and order in his inner sanctuary. There, knowledge becomes possible, in the biblical meaning of the term: a living contact with truth, a transformation in love. An encounter with God.

There is the realm of the sacred Wisdom, inner knowledge of the things of God, taste for the divine realities.

Wisdom gives man the faculty of judging from the very viewpoint of his Creator and Father, his Redeemer, whose love and mercy are infinite and overcome even His justice. She is a spark, in the human heart, of the fire of the heart of God; she is a share in the refreshing breeze of His Spirit.

Elijah was still in the turmoil and noise of his disturbing experience on Mount Carmel: the ordeal ended with the victory of Yahweh and the slaughter of the prophets of

Baal, but also the hatred of the queen of Samaria before which he had had to flee away. Alone, discouraged, his strength had broken down. Then, in the silence of the desert, the Angel of God led him again to the peace of his soul, and he went to meet God. Standing in the hollow of the rock on the holy mountain, the prophet was awaiting the passage of the Lord. Then came

> a great and strong wind overthrowing the mountains and breaking the rocks into pieces; the Lord was not in the wind. And after the wind came an earthquake; the Lord was not in the earthquake. After the earthquake . . . a whistling of a gentle air. . . .[1]

The Lord was in the peace and silence of the gentle breeze. Elijah was freed from his own fear, from his weakness. In the total silence of forty days in the wilderness, he then became a new man. The captivity of his soul had given way to the freedom of a son of God. His chains, broken; his soul in joy.

The ways the divine flame takes possession of the soul are as many as are the ways of the Spirit in the life of man. Sometimes it rushes into it in the roar of a storm. But sometimes the Beloved One embraces the soul in a perfect silence. Always this flame, once lit, is a consuming fire, achieving in the depths a purifying work "as the crucible tests the silver, and the furnace, gold."[2]

Silence and peace are indissolubly bound together. Long is often the pilgrimage, hard the noisy battles between men, and in man's flesh and spirit. Uneasy is the access into the Holy City, the new Jerusalem, where dwells the Glory of God in its eternal Silence.

Dionysius tells us that silence pacifies the mind, makes unity in our faculties, reveals the mysteries of the "theology," more than any natural light. If it is true that any intellectual approach to truth requires freedom of the mind—and that freedom cannot exist amid the thundering noises, and through the turmoil of our passions—so much is it true that any approach to the Ineffable could not be reached but in the depth of a pacified soul, and in the inner silence which allows her to listen. The voice of the Spirit is a whisper; only the prepared ear of the heart could grasp it. Not in the protracted effort of a peaceless inner tension but in the loving attention of a friend who listens to the very silences of his present beloved one.

And in the silence of a long closeness to God is reached this deeper knowledge of the universe which is properly called Wisdom. Only in this silence could we, as sons of God sharing in the mystery of His own life, hear the Word uttered to us by the Father in the Love of the Spirit. "Hearken, son," begins the Rule of St. Benedict. "One word spake the Father, which Word was His Son. And this Word He speaks ever in eternal silence. And in silence must it be heard by the soul."[3] Such is the mystery of God's silence, the exemplary source of man's silence, in the cosmic great silence which awed Pascal and inspired the Oriental poet: "Silence, this God's heart pulsation."[4]

Using the term *peregrinatio,* pilgrimage, voyage (toward the New Jerusalem) to express the deep meaning of monasticism, the Fathers of the Desert gave us these two sayings: *Tacere est peregrinatio* (silence is the pilgrimage); In the mastery over your lips is the departure abroad. It is the *exodus* from slavery toward the possession of the Kingdom. But the long pilgrimage has to go through the great silent aridity of the desert, as if the Lord Himself were often absent, keeping silent.

True silence is a welcome. It has no common grounds with the mutism of a bitter heart, brooding over its resentments, poisoning itself in endless murmuring; and one knows that hatred could keep the lips tightened—the demon is a mute spirit. Neither has it anything in common with the silence of this who, having nothing to give, remains closed in his nullity—or of this who by cowardice does not say the saving word which would free his brother.

These false images of silence do not give God, whose image in man could only be kept and developed through charity, in the total openness of a heart given to God and to his fellowmen, after having rubbed off in the silent process of a long effort his own selfishness. This is the part of the virtue of patience, taken the way the Fathers understood it: a peaceful and silent suffering and mastering of self against one's selfishness, bitterness, anger, hatred. Silence is a strength. "In silence and trust shall be your strength" (Isaiah 30:15).

There is the silence of the great sufferings, of the body or of the soul. It could lead to despair, or to a deepening maturity, a ripening of the fruit of one's inner life at the moment perhaps when the life of the body is more fragile.

> This whom cancer torments, you see him biting his lips and keeping silence: over the turmoil of his flesh his pain is changing into a spiritual tree which grows out its branches and its roots in a realm which is not that of the things, but of the meaning of things.[5]

Silence, writes P. Blanchard, is "a sign of the mystery of man"—man, whose freedom allows him to express himself or to withdraw in himself, "in that inner room which is his paradise, where he purifies himself and finds his own unity."[6]

Peter Minard

NOTES

1. I Kings 19:11–12.
2. Proverbs 27:22.
3. *St. John of the Cross, Counsels of Light and Love.*
4. Dhan Gopal Mukenji.
5. Antoine de Saint-Exupéry, *Citadelle.*
6. *Jacob and the Angel, Etudes carmelitaines* (1957).

THE IMAGINATION

The history of the word has had so many vicissitudes that one has the right, in fact the need, to declare what one means by it. That is what I do, for example, when I declare, for one thing, that the life of the imagination is not the life of fantasy, no matter how inventive or brilliant the latter may be.

One of the great tasks of the imagination—once again as I see it—is to form competent, adequate images of reality, most especially the human reality. Fantasy does the very opposite. It abandons reality and becomes increasingly sterile as it distances itself from the actual or refuses to return periodically to the actual to feed upon it. Therefore it is not true to say that the insane have too much imagination; they have endless fantasy but too little imagination, being unable, as a consequence, to cope with reality. Martin Buber has used the wonderful phrase "imagining the real," and I think this belongs to the very substance of the life of imagining. How true this is will become clearer if we take our examples from the human reality. It is there that we can ask some of the great questions of ourselves, of our imaginations, and of our consciences in the bargain. For our images do not come ready-made, they are not mechanical, they are not arty; rather they are made by ourselves, and most of them take a lifetime to make. What, in the concrete, is our image of a man? What is our image of a woman? What is our image of a child? What is our image of death? What is our image of the human?—is it white, black, small, large, dirty, disgusting? Is it imaged as inside of us, a figment of our thought and our needs, something to be used, therefore, according to our purposes and gratifications? Or is it really there, absolutely independent of me, saying yes and no, demanding to be seen as it is? Or is our image born of *literalism,* the kind of fact-is-a-fact-is-a-fact that would imagine man as a hunk of hair and a rag of bones? What I am reaching to say is that, contrary to many of the understandings of the word, there is nothing more important, more actual, and more scientific than imagination and the true life of the imagination. If the imagination goes, reality goes with it—the reality of man above all. If the imagination goes, then the madmen, who have no imagination, will return, and they will put us all, a hank of hair and a rag of bones, back in Dachau and Buchenwald.

William Lynch

SYMBOL

We know by images. To have a clear idea means to have a clear mental "image." We say "I see!" when we mean "I understand clearly." But there are two distinct though interrelated paths: the discursive and the intuitive approaches; and to these two approaches correspond two kinds of mental images, two kinds of concepts. They differ in their origins.

The intuitive kind has simply grown up in our minds as we ourselves were growing from experience to experience. We are not likely to remember the first incident which sowed the concept in the mind. One day we "discover" it, already deeply rooted in our subconscious, its branches expanding in every direction.

When a word like "water" rings a bell for you, this is so because a thousand long-forgotten experiences have yielded the bell-metal for the founding of this concept. Your first bath; the lawn-sprinkler on the freshly trimmed grass a dripping faucet throughout a long night; rain drumming on the canvas of a tent; the tang of the seashore; thundering breakers; the taste of salt-water; a birdbath; drift ice; the polluted canal; fountains at Salzburg, Rome or Versailles. Gushing, splashing, murmuring.

With every new experience of water this reality grows deeper in color and more profound in meaning. "Water" becomes for us transparent for a mysterious reality which it signifies and which it somehow contains. This happens before we are reflectively aware of it.

The other kind of mental image, the discursive concept, has not sprung up spontaneously, though we are easily deceived on this point. Our mind has constructed this concept as one constructs a schematic drawing on a board. We have arrived at it by a process of discursive reasoning, by analysis, comparison, elimination and composition, and what we have achieved is quite an accomplishment. The concept H_2O would be a typical example. It is useful to us in chemistry precisely because it has been stripped of all that gives fullness to the concept "water."

We need poetry and we need science, and, above all, men who speak both languages. Both concepts will serve us as long as we avoid the danger of confusing them and the danger of forgetting which of them is closer to reality. We are apt to forget that the scientific concept is a drastically impoverished one. The intuitive concept is a living tree, the other a piece of milled lumber.

The symbol is as contradictory as life. If we want manageable precision we must employ metaphor. Symbol is the image itself with every restriction removed from intuition. We invent metaphor, but we discover symbol. Metaphor takes one thing and compares it with another. Ideally there is a one-to-one relationship. The elaborate metaphor of the olive tree in Romans 11:17–24 is an example. Israel is like an olive tree. Those who rejected the Gospel are like branches cut off. The gentiles who come to the faith are like wild olive branches grafted on. But St. Paul assures us that the original branches can be grafted back, and finally the imagery gets strained to the point where one wonders, why bother. All that evidently matters is the thought, and this thought outgrows the image like a costume bursting at the seams.

Unfortunately this is apt to happen; one might even imagine the inspired author commenting to his secretary, "I'm afraid we've killed that metaphor." But no one can kill a symbol.

Take the tree where it appears not as metaphor but as symbol in the Bible. It is there in the beginning, in the middle and in the end: as the tree of Knowledge in the Garden of Eden, as the Tree of Life in the Heavenly Jerusalem, and halfway between the two as the Rood Tree. And between these three pillars the Bible weaves a garland of imagery, from the apple tree to which the Bridegroom is likened in the Song of Songs to the tree of curse on which a criminal is to be hanged according to the Law. Every new reference adds new overtones to the unfolding theme of eating and knowing, of obedience and rebellion, life and death, blessing and curse, all symbolized by the tree. Here nothing can be translated without loss into a different imagery. It is simply held up before us like the wood of the cross on Good Friday: "Ecce . . ."—just look and kneel; that is all. That is all we can do with a symbol, all we need to do.

While metaphor surrounds a garden patch of insight with a handsome hedge, symbol throws open a door of wide outlook and leads us into the great wilds of real life. Here, too, symbol and metaphor parallel intuition and discursive reasoning. Discursively we try to grasp truth, by intuition we lose ourselves in it. The two are mutually complementary like expansion and depth, the two dimensions of our inner growth. Only by retaining the tension between the horizontal and the vertical dimensions can we hope to gain access to truth.

The horizontal dimension is that of the objectively verifiable; the vertical one is the dimension of the subjectively experienced. One demands matter-of-fact dealing and skill, the other wonderment, reverence, awe. In the one we use, in the other we enjoy. In science our knowledge expands in quantity, in poetry our insight deepens in quality. The one, though it be immense, remains finite; the other is by its very essence infinite. As we expand we accumulate material—coded material, as it were—but we must go down into our depth to find the key to that code. Depth is the dimension of meaning.

To find meaning in the world presupposes that we take all things somehow as signs. The world has meaning because it points beyond itself; it comes to us as a word to which we ought to listen, it contains a message which we can understand. Poets and children are aware of this. They may misunderstand the message; but in this, at least, they are right—they realize spontaneously that it is a message. And they realize, too, that it is a message addressed to the whole man, to the heart, the core and center where intellect, will and emotions are still one. The center where I am most truly myself and at the same time most deeply in communion with all other beings and with Mystery as the ground of all being—this is the heart. And the language of the heart is the language of symbol.

David Rast

ETERNITY

The word is sometimes used as a synonym for immortality, or endless future duration in time. But "immortality" or "everlastingness" are clearer labels for this concept. "Eternal" properly implies unborn as well as undying, or without beginning or ending in time. God has been viewed as eternal in this sense by nearly all theologians. Agreement has been less complete as to whether the divine freedom from birth and death implies complete absence of change.

The classical view regarded the divine birthlessness and deathlessness as connoting strict immutability. But the case was not carefully argued. A Socinian theologian rejected the identification of eternal with immutable, and substituted the following: That is eternal which cannot not exist. This was Aristotle's view also. The heavenly bodies, he thought, were eternal but not wholly immutable; however, they, like the truly immutable "unmoved mover," or God, existed by necessity, not contingently. To say God could not fail to exist is one thing; to say He could not fail to exist just as He is is another. Immutability follows from existential existence only on the assumption that one must identify an individual by the totality of its properties, rather than by essential properties as distinguished from accidental ones. Ordinarily we think we can identify our acquaintances without knowing all that may happen to them in the future. Self-identity, or "genetic identity," is compatible with change. It has been shown that the necessary existence of God as God, as identical with himself, is quite compatible with his possessing accidental and hence changeable qualities. (See my books *Anselm's Discovery* and *The Logic of Perfection.*)

The Socinian position is perfectly logical, so far as anyone has yet shown. And it avoids many difficulties (which skeptics and atheists like to stress) inherent in the idea of an immutable yet allegedly conscious and free being. Carneades and, much later, Hume showed how serious these difficulties are. They are not necessary consequences of the religious belief that God is, before and after all, birthless and deathless, nor of the belief that his existence is a necessary, not an accidental, feature of reality.

The famous Boethian definition of the divine eternity, that it is the *totum simul,* the vision of all things in a single immutable intuition or spiritual state, stands or falls with the denial of mutability to God. The alternative is to modify the Boethian idea as follows: At each moment, there is a divine intuition of all past events. This intuition is single or unitary, so far as that totality, that "all," of events is concerned. However, the next moment there is a partly new totality, since additional events have occurred; and this new totality is then embraced in a new *totum simul.* Thus the divine state is ever growing, it acquires additions but suffers no losses. Each item of divine knowledge is immutable, but there is no final totality of items, no final summing up of reality. This is the theological version of the cumulative view of duration which Bergson was perhaps the first to present clearly. Whitehead's "immortality of the past" as "objectified" anew in each new creature, and in ultimate form in each new phase of the Consequent Nature of God, is the first appearance of the doctrine in a powerful metaphysical system. But it was already implicit in Socinian theology. Analogically speaking, God "remembers" all the past; but his vision of the future is limited to those features of coming events which are implied by present causal conditions. The element of freedom in process limits even divine knowledge of the future only because such limitation defines futurity as such. To know the partly open future as simply closed would be to fall into error. Nor does it escape this argument to say, with Aquinas and others, that for God nothing is past or future but all is eternally present. For if events do not exist to be known before they happen, much less do they exist eternally. The Thomistic (or Augustinian) view accentuates the paradox of "foreknowledge" rather than mitigates it.

An essential feature of the Socinian-Bergsonian-Whiteheadian view is that it rejects the association of "mutable" with "corruptible" which dominated the classical tradition. Change is not essentially gain balanced by loss, it is not essentially substitution of one present for another, an oscillation back and forth between privation and possession of properties. "Duration is creation or nothing," said Bergson. Events come into being, are created, but they are not taken out of being or destroyed. Or, as Whitehead put it, actual occasions become, they "do not change" and they are "everlasting." Change is the succession of becomings, each of which embodies, objectifies, its predecessors. In God this preservation of the past is ideally complete.

It is sometimes argued that a past fully preserved is not past but present. I think it can be shown that this is a fallacious argument, since it employs "present" in two senses, the one temporal and the other epistemic. To identify these senses begs the question at issue. Of course the past can be present epistemically, otherwise it would be unknowable. And it can be fully present epistemically if complete knowledge, omniscience, is possible at all.

Charles Hartshorne

ABSOLUTE

This word has been used, alas, for various and in some cases mutually incompatible ideas. Its clearest meaning is "independent," or "neutral to relational alternatives." Thus, if X is absolute, then it makes no difference to X whether or not it is in relation to some other thing, Y, or whether or not Y exists. "Absolute" contrasts with "relative," and the relative is that which is what it is only because something else is what *it* is. The relative is that into which relations to other things enter constitutively. The absolute "is what it is, regardless of anything else," the relative is what it is only with regard to something else.

Confused notions of absoluteness include the following: The absolute is what is in no sense in relation to anything. But since to think about a thing is to make it a term of the relation—thinking about—this definition defines something unthinkable and therefore is useless. The absolute can very well be "in relation"; the point is, the relation is not "in" it. By contrast, relations are in relative things. "Internal" relations define relativity, "external" relations define absoluteness. To say that no relation is external and yet, with F. H. Bradley, for example, to speak of "the absolute" is to talk nonsense. There is absoluteness just in so far as there are external relations.

Another confused definition is, The absolute is all-inclusive, and hence is "not dependent upon anything outside itself." But if anything depends upon other things, a whole depends upon its parts. The parts, to be sure, are in the whole, but nevertheless they are truly "other" than the whole. A man's whole body is not his heart, but it depends upon his heart. Inclusion is one thing, identity is quite another. The all-inclusive whole depends upon everything whatever, and is the least absolute thing conceivable. All relations are in it, and if this does not make it relative, then the term relative is useless.

If the words absolute and relative, or independent and dependent, have meaning, they must get this meaning from experience. One learns to speak of dependence or its negative from examples, and one does not begin this learning with what philosophers call the absolute. We say that a certain writer is independent of another because the second writer published only after the first had ceased to write, or because the writings of the one were not accessible to the other. Thus, so far as the pair of writers is concerned, one is independent or absolute. If the second writer had read the first, then he was not entirely independent of him, and so far as the pair is concerned he was relative, not absolute (though his dependence may have been trivially slight). Of course, neither writer is independent with respect to all other writers. Thus both are relative when the context is sufficiently widened. However, if no writer is independent of every other, equally no writer is dependent upon every other. He has not read all writers other than himself.

From the foregoing we derive a meaning for the absolute as most properly used in philosophy: the entity which is what it is regardless of anything else whatever, or the entity whose relations are exclusively external or nonconstitutive.

Traditionally this was taken to be God (*q.v.*), as wholly independent of the world. But there is a parallel concept which tradition overlooked. Ordinary things, we have seen, are relative to some others and independent of some others. In certain limited contexts they are absolute and in other limited contexts they are relative. But no ordinary thing is either absolute or relative in the universal or cosmic context. A man is not, in any aspect of his individual nature, independent of all other things, nor is he in any aspect dependent upon or influenced by all other things. This yields by contrast two concepts, universal independence and universal dependence, universal absoluteness and universal relativity. If the former is divine, what is the latter? Some writers, including this one, are convinced that both concepts apply to God and to him alone. Since relative and not-relative (or absolute) are contradictories, it may seem logically impossible that both should apply to God. But logicians do not say, "Nothing can be P and not-P." They say, "Nothing can *in the same respect* be P and not-P." Applying this to God, we may without contradiction say, in some respect God is independent of all other things, in some other respect he is dependent upon all.

The question remains as to how the two respects are to be distinguished and related. And what about God as a whole, or taking all aspects into account? Is God in his total reality relative or absolute? Let us look again at the ordinary case of relative and absolute, that is, the application of these terms to limited contexts. If a writer, X, depends for some feature of his writing upon another writer, Y, there will be other features of X not thus dependent. But, since the total reality of the first writer includes the dependent feature, and since a whole depends upon its constituents, the first writer in his total reality will, in the limited context in question, be relative, not absolute. We thus see that relativity, not absoluteness, is the inclusive concept. Universalizing the context gives no ground for reversing this relationship. God, as relative to all things, is God in his totality or fullness. God as independent of all things is only a partial aspect of deity.

The two aspects can be clearly distinguished with respect to the attribute of omniscience. God depends upon the creatures for his knowledge that they exist as they do. For were they not to exist, or to exist otherwise, then God would not know them to exist as in fact they do, but would know them to be as they would, on the hypothesis, be. God's actual knowledge of the particular world which exists is a relative feature of the divine reality. But what is not relative is the abstract property of being omniscient. For no matter what world, say W, exists, God is sure, without possible failure, to know that this is so. Thus "W exists" implies "God knows that W exists," and "God knows that W exists" implies "W exists." This relation of God's knowing to any possible world constitutes his omniscience. But the relation itself is an abstraction. God's merely being omniscient is simply the common denominator of all possible divine states in relation to possible world states; it is the principle that there will without fail be knowledge in God appropriate to the state of the world. That God is all-knowing under any possible circumstances is a truth independent of alternative world states. But that he knows that you or I exist is not independent of our existence. So the concrete reality of the divine knowing is relative to the creatures; but the abstract perfection which is the necessary and eternal prerogative of God's way of knowing is independent of the creatures.

What tradition mistook for the actuality of God, for God in his fullness, was but an extremely abstract characteristic of that actuality. The simply independent or absolute God is an abstract or conceptual entity (God himself has this concept, and much more clearly than we); but the actual divine life in its concreteness is the only thing there is which is relative to all things whatsoever. The inclusive divine attribute is not absoluteness but Transcendental Relativity (symbolized as R), sensitivity not to some but to any and every relational alternative. This is the divine love for the world.

Among the less clear interpretations of "absolute" is that which takes it as synonymous with "perfect" in the sense of a "sum of all perfections" or *ens realissimum*, the exhaustive realization of possible value. This view implies that in any relevant dimension of value the absolute being attains the possible maximum. It follows that, if there are any dimensions of worth in which a maximum is impossible, a simply absolute being must have *no* value on such a dimension. And there are such dimensions, as Leibniz, for one, saw clearly. For instance, magnitude has no absolute maximum, nor (as he proved) has velocity. Indeed, quantity generally has none. Leibniz, being among those who identified the absolute with the exhaustive realization of possible value, had to deny that quantity has ultimate relevance as measure of value. The absolute was "simple." And yet we normally use degree of complexity as positive index of worth. A musical chord is as harmonious as a symphony; it is merely less complex. Beauty, as unity in variety, has no maximal possibility, since this would have to be an unsurpassable variety integrated in an unsurpassably harmonious whole. But given any variety, there could be a greater, since all possible variety would be confusion (see *God*). So aesthetic value cannot be absolute. Yet, what would life or value be without harmony? It follows that the supremely valuable cannot be in all respects absolute, the realized sum of possible perfections or *ens realissimum*. Absolute is a negative term, the absence of dependence, but supreme value is as positive a term as possible; the two are far from synonymous. In those dimensions of value which permit a maximum, the absolute entity will attain this maximum, since otherwise it would not be immune to increase, and it is not intelligible that this increase should have no dependence upon other things. In the remaining aspects the supremely valuable being (see *God*)—which it is utterly confusing to call "the absolute"—will have aspects which are unsurpassable by another, and yet not unsurpassable by itself. This can be shown to fit the requirements of Transcendental Relativity, R.

Charles Hartshorne

GOD

The term is most properly used to denote the object of worship in the high religions. Worship itself means unstinted devotion, or love "with all one's mind and heart and soul and strength." Traditionally (in the West especially) it was held that only what is in all respects "perfect," hence incapable of any kind of increase or addition, could be deserving of worship. Hence God was declared immutable, timeless, unlimited, independent, absolute, cause of all but effect of nothing, influencing all but influenced by nothing. However, another view has been gaining ground in recent centuries and especially in recent decades. To be worshipful, God must be exalted above all possible rivals, he must be unsurpassable *by others*. What was generally overlooked, however, was that this formula does not of itself exclude that God may surpass himself. To be surpassed by another is indeed a position not to be thought of as possible for God; but it seems quite possible that a being could be surpassable, though by himself only. If God could be surpassed by another, then we must, at least potentially, worship this other and not God. But if God surpasses himself, this need not exalt anyone else to the divine level. Thus, suppose that God without possible failure knows all truth, whereas any other being has only uncertain and partial grasp of truth. Even so, if there is genuine creation, or becoming of new items of reality, and consequently new truths to be known each moment, then God, although never failing to know any part of the truth, will acquire new knowledge from moment to moment, but only so far as there are new truths to be known. Lesser beings are constantly learning old truths which we previously failed to acquire and are constantly shedding errors about old matters of fact. Any alleged rival to God could be distinguished from him only by partial ignorance or error. Thus divine growth does not imply the possibility of a rival to God, and hence it is compatible with his worshipfulness.

One of the first to realize the foregoing was Fechner. The perfection of God, he held, is the unique excellence of his manner of increase, not the exclusion of all increase.

But still, it may seem that a being capable of additional value must "lack" something and so not deserve unstinted admiration. The fallacy in this Platonic argument is so subtle that more than two thousand years went by before it was clearly exposed. It is assumed, without good ground, that the notion of an unsurpassable maximum of value, or "sum of all possible perfections," is a self-consistent idea. If there could be such a maximum, then indeed God to deserve worship must embody it. For, if the maximum were possible and God did not have it, the possible possessor of the maximum would be a possible superior to God. But if the maximum is not possible, God's not having it is irrelevant. It is no "defect" to lack that the idea of which is nonsense. Does the idea of an unsurpassable maximum make sense? There is good reason to doubt it. There are mutually incompatible but genuine values, good things possible separately but not in combination. Every artist must exclude possible beauties from his work if it is to have definite beauty. The cosmic artist is not, so far as we can see, in a different position. He cannot have all possible worlds as all actual; for this would be sheer confusion or indefiniteness. Thus, for example, the laws of nature are definite only because they exclude other possible laws. Any world order represents an arbitrary choice; all possible orders would be no order. God must renounce something when he makes creative decisions about the world. He must also lose something when the creatures make decisions. God is the God of the world the creatures have helped to make by their free decisions; he is not, but might have been, the God of the worlds he or the creatures might have made by deciding otherwise.

One can hold that the world is nothing to God, so that the exclusion of possible worlds from actualization implies no loss for him. But then God lacks what even we have, the ability to love others and enjoy their happiness. He lacks the very best thing we know, sympathy or love in any intelligible sense. And why should God know the world if it is nothing to him; or what is knowledge but realistic evaluation?

Two great men, Spinoza and Leibniz, tried to reconcile the idea of the immutable perfection of God with the existence of the world. Spinoza did it by holding that the absolute infinity of God's power is expressed in an absolute infinity of his creation. He has actually all possible value; for all possible creatures exist somewhere somehow. But then "possible" and "actual" coincide, freedom is the same as necessity, and so on through a long list of paradoxes. Spinoza can give no reason whatever for denying the possibility of many things which we have every reason to believe are not actual. Leibniz had a different paradox. He held that while not all possible worlds are actual, the actual world is the best of the possible ones; and so God's immutable perfection is fully expressed in his creating it. But then, since God's wisdom and power are perfect, his creating the best possible world represents not one among possible divine choices but the only possible choice. He could not have decided to create a lesser world instead of the best one. Yet, as Leibniz on occasion says himself, a possible world is simply one that could result from divine action. So the so-called possible worlds are really impossible, and the best possible is the only possible world. Again we have a collapse of the contrast between actual and possible.

What these great intellects could not do, no one else has succeeded in doing either. There is reason to doubt the legitimacy of the alleged idea of absolute perfection. If it is a pseudo-idea, then it need not be considered in construing the attributes of God as deserving of worship. We do not worship God because he is something nonsensical; and we should not refuse to worship him because he "fails" to be that something. God is unsurpassably perfect so far as surpassability by another is concerned; but there is no need to suppose him unsurpassable absolutely and with respect to all dimensions of value.

If God can acquire additional value by actualizing additional world-possibilities, or having the creatures actualize them for him, he is not in every respect independent of the world. He is not what philosophers call the absolute (*q.v.*), cause of all things, effect of nothing, influencing all but influenced by none. Rather, he is both universal cause and universal effect. It has too seldom been noted that what makes one being superior to another is not that the one influences and the other is influenced. The higher animals are influenced in many more ways than the lower; and this greater scope of sensitivity to influence is the key to their greater scope of influence over others. Our forefathers seemed oddly insensitive to the claims of sensitivity as a merit.

God is the universal being, or universally influenced, universally exerting influence, universally loving and universally loved (however unconsciously), surpassing all (including himself), the sole rightful object of worship.

The foregoing doctrine has been called *panentheism,* also the *neoclassical* view of God. Those who have most closely approximated it include Faustus Socinus and his followers, Fechner the German psychologist, Lequier and Bergson in France, Varisco in Italy, Montague, Brightman, Hocking, and Whitehead in the United States. The present writer seems to be the only one who has paid much attention to the history of the view and the only one who has expounded it at great length.

The idea of God may be variously related to the following: the eminently independent reality or the *absolute;* the eminently *valuable* reality; the all-inclusive reality or *whole;* the eminently *relative* reality. These may be symbolized respectively by A, V, W, R. Using G for God, the object of worship, loving and worthy of being loved by all persons, the various views may be summed up in the formulae which follow.

I. $G=V=W=R(A)$
$G \neq A$

God is the eminently valuable, all-inclusive, and relative reality, with an aspect of eminent absoluteness; he is not identical with the absolute. Neoclassical theism or panentheism. Implied in primitive Judaism, Christianity, Islam, Zoroastrianism, Confucianism? Also by Plato's Timaeus, perhaps.

II. $G=V=A$
$G \neq W$

God is the eminently valuable reality and is the absolute, but not the all-inclusive whole. Medieval Judaism, Christianity, Islam.

III. $G \neq V$
$V=A=W(?)$

God (*Isvara,* "the Lord") is eminently valuable only in the semi-real stance of Maya; the supremely valuable from the truest perspective is the absolute, which is the whole only in the sense that what seems outside it (the relative) is not fully real. Hinduism in its orthodox philosophical interpreters, especially Sankara. Tendencies toward I, II or III occur, but are seldom clearly carried through.

IV. $V=W=Ar$
$G?$ $R?$

The eminently valuable reality is all-inclusive and is a mysterious nonconceptualizable union of the absolute and ordinary things. Neither God nor eminent relativity seems to be recognized. Buddhism.

According to Leibniz, metaphysicians err in what they deny, not in what they assert. The signs for inequality in

II and III are essentially negations; for they imply that God fails to have supreme value or to embrace all reality in himself. (The world which is posited as outside God must have some value—or what does the word "value" mean?—yet this value is attributed not to God, but only to a strange totality, "God and the world," which thus becomes a super-reality of which God and world are both only constituents. The omission of both God and eminent relativity from IV is in effect a negation. What about the inequation in I? It is essentially positive, since its effect is only to make it possible to assert both the eminent independence and the eminent dependence or sensitive responsiveness of God. All our experience supports the view that such responsiveness is positive, not a mere privation. Actually, the inequation in I is already covered by the positive meanings of the fourfold equation. By contrast, in II the inequation results not from the positive use of eminent worth or absoluteness to characterize God, but from the implicit denial of eminent relativity. Similarly in III the necessity to deny the ultimate worth of God is a consequence of identifying this worth with "the absolute" as devoid of eminent relativity, and also of genuine inclusiveness (since it is a Pickwickian inclusion which does away with the included). As for IV, Buddhism, it does not deny anything explicitly perhaps, but implicitly it denies both God and eminent relativity.

Thus all the positive content inherent in the basic conceptions is acknowledged in I, which by Leibniz's criterion, whose validity this writer accepts, must be truer than its chief traditional rivals.

It is notable that whereas in Europe for many centuries God was identified with the absolute, and as definitely distinguished from the whole of reality, in Asia scarcely anyone simply identified the religious idea with the philosophical concept of absoluteness, and few identified the supremely valuable reality with but one real element of the whole, however preeminent this element.

That missionaries from the West fared so ill in the Orient may stem in no small part from these two great differences, especially since in both cases it is Asia which thought the more correctly. The God of religion cannot be the absolute, nor can he fail to include all things in his knowledge and hence in his own reality. The known is not outside the adequate knowledge of it, nor the knowledge outside the knower.

On the other hand, why should the West accept the paradox that the worshipful reality, God, is not the supreme reality? Or the paradox that the entire world of individuals responding to one another and to God is not really a diversity of individuals at all, so that, for instance, the philosopher only seems to exist and to hold this or that view about God and the absolute, and there only seems to be a difference between having and not having the truth about reality, since there is just reality knowing itself, or just knowledge as such—or however the paradox is put? Asia can give no genuine reason for either of these paradoxes except that they somehow (highly ambiguously, in fact) receive support from venerated writings. This is the same inconclusive reason given for the two Occidental paradoxes spoken of above. All four paradoxes are absent from View I, and yet all the basic ideas except the utterly evasive idea of Maya (neither real nor unreal) are affirmed in that view.

In both Occident and Orient certain philosophers asserted the right to identify their doctrines with prephilosophical scriptures. In both cases it is decidedly controversial whether or not the doctrines fit the religious documents any better, or even as well, as View I would do. But since this view did not exist as a clear-cut philosophical doctrine, no one tried to read it into the sacred writings. Philo, Maimonides, Augustine, Al-Ghazali, Sankara, Ramanujan—these and countless more did not hesitate to make the prophets or religious founders responsible for their own philosophical insights or oversights.

God is not to be *defined* as the absolute, though he is (in the appropriate respects) absolute, nor as the infinite, though he is (in the appropriate aspects) infinite, nor as the perfect, though he is (in the appropriate aspects) perfect. Rather, God is by definition worshipful, and this means exalted beyond all possible rival or superior. He is not to be equaled or surpassed *by another,* hence in those respects in which value cannot admit a maximum he is surpassable, and perpetually surpassed, by himself alone. The self-surpassing aspects are the eminently relative ones, R; the aspects unsurpassable even by God himself are the eminently independent or absolute ones, A. But since the relative includes the absolute, the formula is R(A). Transcendent Relativity is divinity itself, the love which cherishes all contingent and changing existence, not the independence which is neutral to existential alternatives or changes. There is such independence in God—*in* God but yet not simply God, not his very divinity.

Charles Hartshorne

SHAPE? IMAGINATION? LIGHT? FORM? OBJECT? COLOR? WORLD?

SHAPE?

Good shape, bad shape, outlines, edges?
Absolute shape, square?
Horizontal, vertical shapes? Trisections?
Circle as shape, shape as circular, target, sun?
Bull's-eye, God's-eye? Shape of time?
Circular heavens above, endlessness?
Square as shapelessness.

IMAGINATION?

Imagining? Imaging? Imagery? Image?
Imaginary-museum, image of timelessness?
Image of emptiness, empty image?
Imaginationless, fantasyless, surrealistless?
Imagelessness.

LIGHT?

Harsh, soft, reflected, absorbed, transparent light?
Soft lights, sweet music, sweeter unheard music?
Frozen-music architecture? Gothic-Greek light?
Twilight-light, twilight-time, twilight space?
Broken, baroque, dissolved light?
Iridescence, evanescence, transcendence light?
Luminous-numinous? Rome-versus-East light?
Darkness, grayness, greyness, dullness light?
Lightlessness.

FORM?

Spirit, spirit of forms, forms of forms?
Form of forms, formalism, uniform? One form?
Style-cycles, archaic, classic, late forms?
Broken-forms, impressionism, empty forms?
Bad form, good form, right, wrong form?
Form follows function-filthy-lucre?
Form without substance? Without end? Without time?

OBJECT?

Subject, objective, non-objective, non-subjective?
Object of art, object-art, op-art? Antique?
Subjectlessness, matterlessness, thinglessness?
Objectlessness.

COLOR?

Red, white, blue, flying colors?
Green, orange, purple, glossy-black?
Black as color, black as non-color, no-color?
Colorfulness, color interest?
Interest is of no interest in art.

Art-of-color versus art-of-painting?
Color-engineering, color-psychology?
Color-symbolism, symbolic-color, colored-symbols?
Colored crayons, chalks, markers?
Prism, spectrum, rainbow? Color-field?
Race-color, rat-race, dogma-eat-dogma, holy cats?
Topcat, birds of a color feather together?
Horse of a different color?
Hue, tone, tint, tinge, dye, shade, glow, flush, key?
Pigment, wash, distemper, stain, grain, daub?
Pure, primary, primitive, barbaric, emblazon?
Local-color, value, disguise, flesh, blush?
Broken-color, baroque-color, polychromatism?
Full, high, knee-deep, wet, dry, hard, soft, near, far color?
True to one's colors? Guilt-edge, blue-chip?
Color as anti-art.

Monochrome, tone down, wash out, bleach, blanch?
Discolored, pallor, pallid, pale?
Dull, cold, muddy, leaden, wan, dun, sallow?
Dead, dingy, ashen, lack-lustre?
Blackness, darkness, chiaroscuro?
Jet, ink, ebony, coal, pitch, soot, charcoal, ivory, lamp?

Right and wrong, wrong color, makes-no-difference?
Colorlessness.

WORLD?

World of art, art-world, world-art?
Best of all possible worlds?
Primary-world, secondary-world?
Free, non-servile, fine, non-applied world?
Pure, ideal, intellectual, useless, timeless world?
Art-world, ivory-tower, control-tower, art-control?
Wheelers-dealers-world? Collectors-world?
Art-words-world, art-critics, art-critters world?
World of business-before-pleasure and vice-versa?
Living, living-it-up, living-it-down, art-world?
Art whorls, whirls, whoreo-heros, parts, rolls?
Painting is more than the scum of its pots?
Can't you tell your impasto from a holy ground?
Holy smoke.

World-art, all-art, all-of-art, universal-art?
Museum-world, museology, museum-without-walls?
World-of-color-slides, images, pictures, signs, symbols?
Wonders-of-the-world, world-travel, wonder of art?
Wonderful world of Disneyland?
World of imagelessness, voices of silence?
Action-arts speak louder than voids.

The-other-world, this-world, second-hand-world?
Day-in-day-out-day-to-day-routine, ritual-world?
Inner-world, all-in-the-mind, nothing-out-there?

Outside-world, world-outside-window, watch out?
Anti-world, anti-matter, anti-texture?
Other-worldly, anti-worldling, anti-happening?
Out-of-this-world world, the other side of creation?
Worldlylessness.

Ad Reinhardt

World

The new discoveries in archeology and paleontology stretch the history of this planet back millions of years. The new discoveries in astronomy and the new movement of humans from this planet into space have extended the scan of man into worlds beyond worlds. Therefore, "world" has ceased to have the limited meaning it once had in connection with the earth on which the human race is very generally thought to have been born. There may be humans in other worlds; for the moment that is still speculation. In any event, a dismaying aspect of the almost infinite stretching of the concept "world" is the diversion of the thought concerning the human being as an individual entitled to liberty as well as equality. "Look in your heart and write," Goethe once remarked. The world of hope for man and woman lies within them. This inner world has not become any less important because of the swelling that has taken place in the idea of world, as that word is usually used. It is only by the rediscovery by the individual of the integrity of his inner life that men and women can hope to humanize any of the new worlds that have been opened to them.

John Nef

FRIENDSHIP

Memory clutches almost wildly, often madly wildly, at the time (perhaps one more idyllic dream?) when sounds of such a word evoked extended visions of all the quietness and all the deep, safe joys for which our weariness ached and sought through every jangled day.

I heard of friendship and remembered (or desired?) soft, suggestive passings of the hands or lips against the hoping flesh and spirit of my life. I heard of friendship and listened longer as it spoke of all the space this being yet needed to cultivate the broad inviolate and dimly sensed savannas of my heart without the fear of heavy-breathing forces of the day breaking down the tender tissues of this often fearful soul. I dreamed the word and found it offered freely all the distance that integrity demands and all the love-warmed grapplings of the night when chills of frightened isolation almost seemed to freeze my mind.

Against such crystal-like remembrances now come the shattering bestial pain of each fresh batch of new friends who blare their love in megawatts and stretch their ritual of dogged affection across the channels of our pain. "Friendly Bob Adams" and "friendly Steve Smith" and "friends" at the bank and "friends" in the store tear at the tissues of our life, and every announcement of their concern points garish neon signs at the twisted sources of our strange despair. Friendship pierces at our minds, demanding poisoned light for each safe and darkened altar of our life, crushing our desires into all the agonies of our hell.

Now I hear of friendship (against my newest will) from the soft and smiling lips of the well-fed multitudes who arrogantly know that by their very whiteness pure friendship must be acknowledged and declared. These are the friends who know with metric certainty when I have pushed too hard against the barriers of my hurt, who announce with perfect un-drawls the daily incantation of the limits of my hope, who know when I have had enough of those elusive human joys to fortify my yearning soul for yet another hundred years of pain. And their kindly passing by my flesh leaves scars eternity in depth. Such is the friendship of this hour.

But scars like these are nothing more than indentations of the mind compared to that unending and unannounced procession of the programmed wounds poured out by friends who poison water and kill the plants, send pious fire against children's fears and order great expansive spears of jagged pain into the waiting wombs of all the East. And the demons seem triumphant as with stereo announcements friendship is proclaimed from whirling dervishes in the sky. Then the word is made steel in the desecration of each inch of land and of each heart that yet remains available to outrage and to love.

So the inviolate places are removed and the cruel distance is soon covered well by tanks and open graves, and the chill of isolation gives way to the acrid burnings of our hell, and friendship is death, deliverance from existence, and the mad dream that once we dreamed seems like a vision of paradise, forever lost. Against the weight of such friendship even the resurrection may not prevail.

Vincent Harding

MARRIAGE

Marriage is the condition of life between man and woman most adequately symbolized by the act of sexual intercourse. It is also the condition irrepressibly mocked and laughed at, not only in revenge against demands that are daily, concrete, and down-to-earth, but also because the employment of its basic symbol requires a fundamental awkwardness and angularity. If we suppose that God (or the dim sources of our biological evolution) wished to play a practical joke on our species, could He have invented a more ungainly way by which human beings might express their love? Marriage, then, is the butt of many jokes, an irrepressible font of complaints, a fecund source of ribaldry and delight, and an agony of too much beauty and comfort, too much anger and despair.

In our society, marriage is ordinarily monogamous, although serial polygamy is permitted. Monogamous marriage appears to be, generally, a vaguely unhappy arrangement: one can tell how long couples have been married by how far apart they sit in an automobile, or how silent they are at a table for two in a restaurant. Yet it also appears to summon from ordinary men and women the persistence and stability that make marriage one of the most stable of all institutions in our culture. Perhaps, then, David Hume was wrong when he said that since in every life the portion of sadness outweighs that of happiness, to be married is to increase one's unhappiness.

Surely, moreover, a splendid ignorance about sexual happiness characterizes American husbands and wives; at least, so one must conclude from the eagerness with which Americans purchase "how to" books. Can there ever have been a race that advertised it more and enjoyed it less? One wonders, also, whether it is the American male or the American female that is more sexless—although a study of the male characters in the fiction in leading women's magazines, and a study of the female characters in the stories in men's magazines, suggest that the American difficulty might be merely a total imaginative misapprehension of each other. In any case, as long as more male passion, roughly calculated, goes into watching pro football on television than into gently seducing the Mrs., and so long as the lady of the house secretly yearns for a tenderness she no longer seems to attract, the American ship of marriage sails near dangerous rocks. (Americans—as movie censorship and television schedules show—fear sexual involvement but flirt blissfully with murder and violence.)

Technologists continue to suggest that education and technique (more refined measurements, perhaps even certain electronic guidance systems) will do the trick. But old-fashioned theorists counsel plenty of chatter, interchange, emotional involvement in one another's projects, and as much time as possible lying awake together and talking. For the symbol of marriage is an insistent moral imperative. It says that man and woman are two in one flesh. But it is a hard job really to become one; it is even a little terrifying. Everyone, naturally, wants love, but the real thing, when it arrives, is cruel, disconcerting, and frightening. One's partner refuses merely to be an object, a thing, an impersonal presence, and demands one's precious time, careful reflection, and emotional entanglement. It is a dangerous thing to pledge one's unity with another, and perhaps that is why it can be done only by civil prescription. For teen-agers it should be marked "poison," and the shelf on which it is stored should be beyond the reach of the unprepared.

The human person is not, moreover, an atomic "I" but a "we," a member of a family and of a society. Hence, it is not surprising that marriage is hardly ever a strictly personal affair. The family of the bride and the family of the groom are also implicated, and the whole mesh of society grows slightly more ensnarled; marriages often make money for lawyers.

They also help out doctors. For, not infrequently, by accident or by design, children are born in wedlock and, as anybody knows, babies cost money. However, not enough people in our society tell the young how morally important and how joyous it is to have children. In our society, where the myth of romantic love is more powerful than any other, young people are not encouraged to look upon children as a source of crucial personal development; children are, in this view, a hindrance and a distraction. Yet to become a father is different from not having been one; to become a mother involves resources never before called upon. Words like liberty and responsibility take on a new meaning on the other side of that educational threshold. Not only idols, but also parents, have clay feet. After a few mistakes, forgiveness of others becomes a little easier of attainment; and the risk involved in dealing with the lives of other people becomes painfully clear.

There is a justifiably increasing fear, however, of what Barbara Ward once described as thundering herds of pattering feet. Catholic couples, whose Church at this date remains officially firm but in practice divided regarding techniques of responsible parenthood, might well be worried less about the population were it not exploding in their own home. Official decisions of the Church cannot, unfortunately, be retroactive.

Marriage, in short, is a condition of immediate communication, intolerable for sheer joy when communication is acute, more intolerable than anything on earth when communication falls silent. Most marriages, in fact, seem to settle for a more or less peaceful coexistence, which may after all be the source of that political policy which some people desire for the entire world—a kind of cosmic, bored familiarity in which everyone watches television, and lives and lets live.

Michael Novak

PURITY

"Father, I have sinned against purity." The frequent use of this discreet and decorous cliché in the confessional has eventually brought the word "purity" into a kind of discredit from which no intervention of ours, however zealous, can rescue it today. It remains only for us to see what the expression may signify, to consider the misunderstandings that can arise from it and to suggest that there are, after all, other possible meanings to be remembered. But first let us begin with the "sin against purity." Is the very concept of a "sin against purity" perhaps itself a sin against purity? Does it convey an implicit falsification of certain important aspects of human nature? Does it make the whole question of sex impossibly confusing?

Let us inquire into what is meant here by "pure" and "impure." We are at once confronted with a grave semantic misfortune. A refinement of juridical hair-splitting (fortunately unknown to most penitents) has reduced the concept of purity to a very elusive and complex one. The erection that occurs spontaneously without forethought is not impure, or at any rate is "less impure" than one which is deliberately induced by looking at a picture of the Queen of Burlesque, but this on the other hand suddenly becomes less impure or indeed pure if the looker is a moral theologian hunting down an interesting case in the line of duty. In the long run, whether you are pure or not seems to depend on who your lawyer is.

In any event the concept of purity tends to be compounded of two elements. The pure is the asexual and the anesthetic. Man is "pure" when he either has no sexual reactions at all, or when he does not enjoy them, or when he would rather not have them, or when he has done his best to make them hateful and frustrating, or when they are strictly in the line of duty (marital intercourse). To have a slight velleity for sexual pleasure is a bit impure. To get an erection is more so. To touch sexual organs—one's own or those of others—is still more so. To have an orgasm is more so. This whole attitude of abstraction, of hatred and denigration of the body, has finally led to a pathological and totally unrealistic obsession with bodily detail. The custom of penitential tariffs, which goes back to the Irish monastic codes of the High Middle Ages, has, so to speak, "priced" the various acts and parts of the body with appropriate penalties, and this has resulted in a dreadful atomization of love. One could go on at length to develop this idea—not confined to religion, by any means—in which love puts the human body on the market, either as a desirable package of commodities and pleasures or as a highly dangerous compound of moral evils. Love becomes no longer an expression of the communion between persons but a smorgasbord of the senses in which one selects what he wants—or what he thinks he can get away with. Unfortunately, this creates a very special kind of mentality which enables certain persons to manage an aborted sex life as follows: When you have sexual velleities mentally, you cancel them out by saying you don't want them (but you go on having them). As to the rest, just be careful that if they happen they are always accidents, and in order to reassure yourself on this point, make certain that they always take place in some manner that is extremely frustrating, humiliating and unpleasant, or at least inconvenient, so you can be sure you did not "want" them with full deliberation—nobody in his right mind would. Yet, do not ask the question: Are you in your right mind? Let it suffice that you have "preserved your purity."

Would it be too much to recommend a revision of the notion of purity that would enable people to stay fully human?

It will readily be seen that this decadent concept of purity, which has lost all Christian character whatever, depends on a certain stereotyped view of man and of the world. It would be unfair to distinguish this view by calling it Neoplatonic, for it is only the exhausted remnant of a once-living and sophisticated world view. But in any event the typical style it takes is one in which matter is discredited; sense, passion and emotion are feared and detested; purity is associated with spirit or perhaps more crudely with the "mental" and the "intentional" or the "volitive." A dash of pseudo-stoicism will make this a totally voluntaristic exercise. One crushes sense with an act of will. Add a little Jansenism and Manichaeism and you can concoct a gruesome dose of self-hate and loathing for the flesh. This can also combine with a lusty fascination with all forms of "impurity" and even a regular cult of sin, which, of course, takes the righteous form of sin-hunting, censoriousness, planting figleaves on statues and banning obscene movies—of which there are doubtless more than enough. After all, the manias of the pure have contributed to the development of a very special kind of impurity, the salaciousness that always goes as far as a code permits while suggesting all that an average vulgar imagination can conjure up without effort.

What must frankly be said about this perverse conception of purity is that in reality it does nothing at all to bring sexual desire under the control of a free and mature intelligence, in the service of the highest good of human persons. On the contrary, a morbid, unreasonable and prurient approach to sex only degrades and perverts the sexual instinct, leading it into forms of expression which, in their sado-masochism and hypocritical selfishness, are far more dangerous, much more radically "impure" than the normal expression of erotic love. This pessimistic and negative concept of purity tends in the end to a cult of gloom, a hatred of life, and worse still, to a systematic effort to degrade and destroy one of the most precious of God's gifts to man. The result of this degradation can never be the flowering of a "more spiritual" and more self-sacrificing love, but only a shameful and destructive counterfeit.

It is, of course, true that many honest and well-meaning men and women have, through God's mercy, become saints through the suffering imposed on them by their inhuman concept of love—held in perfectly good faith. But let us not say they were sanctified *by* this concept. They were sanctified *in spite* of it.

Platonism is blamed, not without reason, for some of the exaggerations of the view we have described. But let us not forget that Platonism has to be seen in its own social and cultural context, which is not that of our day.

The ancient Platonic view of purity, which possessed a certain distinction of its own, was aristocratic and contemplative. It associated the purity of the "theoretical" mind with leisure that was not defiled by workaday concerns and with speculation which was able to rise above the limitations of matter. In this context the "pure" mind was that which was not bound to images and material concepts but rose freely to the realm of pure ideas and essences, unimpeded by any obstacle. The pure mind was detached, tranquil, not easily distracted. In some contexts this purity was mathematical and scientific. In others, aesthetic. Or in others, ethical. The early Christian monastic tradition, with its emphasis on "purity of heart," applied this Platonic scheme to the Christian contemplative life and to the search for "mystical theology" or union with God beyond all concepts and created essences in the dark night of pure contemplation.

Since in this tradition it was generally understood that involvement both in manual labor and in the sexuality of married life tended to be an obstacle to contemplation, it was assumed that work, married love and active concerns of civic life were less "pure" than the leisure and abstraction of the theoretic life. In order to seek this "purity," ascetics even left the world altogether and fled into the nakedness of the desert where there were the fewest possible obstacles to the direct ascent of the mind to God. This was the pure life par excellence, the *bios angelikos*, or the life of the angels (which are, of course, "pure spirits").

It may be mentioned here that the concept of Platonic love—a purely spiritual eroticism—was also highly sophisticated and complex, and must be seen in the climate of an aristocratic culture in which *eros* was by no means left systematically disincarnate! Unfortunately, this idealism did tend to make a drastic separation between the love of the ideal woman (spiritual) and the love of a prostitute or mistress (fleshly and passionate).

We have now examined two concepts of purity, one of which is morally decadent, the other of which, though noble and respectable, is antiquated and presupposes an entirely different world view from that in which we live. Can the concept of purity be salvaged at all for our time?

To begin with, is it worth salvaging? This depends on what you are trying to save and restore. Obviously, there is no point in brushing up a dusty and rather dreadful old bit of ethical furniture and putting it back in the living room with the Mondrians and the mobile. But on the other hand there is a certain ideal of human integrity in love and in life which was once served by this notion, and can perhaps be served again. Here we must, of course, get rid of all confusion between "purity" and mere respectability or even decency. The existentialists have, in fact, opened up a fairly useful approach to this problem, and if we see that in their idea of the *authentic* use of human freedom they have salvaged some of the value under consideration, we can appreciate what "purity" might conceivably mean for us. Mechanically speaking, we will arrive at this, not by *dividing* as the Platonists did, but by amalgamating, integrating, bringing together. The area in which this most needs to be done is, of course, that of sexual love.

For example, instead of saying that an act is pure when

you *remove* all that is material, sensuous, fleshly, emotional, passionate, etc., from it, we will, on the contrary, say that a sexual act is pure when it gives a rightful place to the body, the senses, the emotions (conscious and unconscious), the special needs of the person, all that is called for by the unique relationship between the two lovers, and what is demanded by the situation in which they find themselves. The aim is not to establish in the stuffiest possible way the full legality of their act of love, but to liberate in them all the capacity for love and for the expression of love that would be truly and fully authentic in their peculiar circumstances. And this, of course, would be decided not exclusively by abstract legal norms (which nevertheless have their objective function and their role in guiding the individual), but also by personal conscience and decision in the light of grace and of the providential demands of one's love.

Here it must be very clearly stated that an uninhibited erotic love between married persons not only can be pure but will most probably be *more pure* than an anguished, constrained and painful attack by an embarrassed husband on his patient and inert wife. The act of sexual love should by its very nature be joyous, unconstrained, alive, leisurely, inventive and full of a special delight which the lovers have learned by their experience to create for one another. There is no more beautiful gift of God than the little secret world of creative love and expression in which two persons who have totally surrendered to each other manifest and celebrate their mutual gift. It is precisely in this spirit of celebration, gratitude and joy that true purity is found. The pure heart is not one that is terrified of *eros*, but one that with the confidence and abandon of a child of God accepts this gift as a sacred trust, for sex, too, is one of the talents which Christ has left us to trade with until He returns. Properly understood sexual union is an expression of deep personal love and a means to the deepening, perfecting and sanctifying of that love. To seek sexual gratification as an end in itself and without due regard for the needs of one's partner would make this true purity of love impossible. Therefore, it is immediately apparent that the notion of purity in love can be fully guaranteed only by a maturely developed sense of personal sacrifice for the good of the other and in order to meet the deepest and most challenging demands of the situation. Here the purity of love will be discovered not by the mechanical application of merely external norms, but by a wise and even inspired integration of personal freedom and objective demands, so that the act of love will flower into a more fruitful and creative expression of life and truth. Such purity must, of course, be judged objectively, not merely by the subjective needs and desires of the lovers, and the standard of objective judgment will be, for instance, the *wholeness* of the act of love. That act will be pure which in all its aspects can be said to respect the truth and integrity, the true needs and the deepest good of those who share it together as well as the objective demands of others, of society and so on.

By this standard, certain casuistical interpretations which would permit an unhealthy and truncated sexual activity as still legally "pure" will be seen as an affront to the authentic wholeness and purity of man. Others which might from a certain point of view shock and scandalize conventional minds may nevertheless meet a profoundly authentic and spiritual demand for inner purity and wholeness. But we cannot say that the individual person is left entirely to his own judgment in each case. The last court of appeal is not subjective freedom, which can easily become arbitrary and lead to just as many appalling truncations as legalism does. The mark of love is its respect for reality and for truth and its deep concern for the values which it must foster, preserve and increase in the world. Such concern is not compatible with fantasy, willfulness, or the neglect of the rights and needs of other people.

In this new approach to purity the emphasis will be not so much on law as on love, not so much on what happens to nature or to the parts of the body as to what develops in the person (though in this case the two are manifestly inseparable). We must consider not so much what is acceptable in a social milieu as what will truly provide a creative and intimately personal solution to the questions raised in each special case.

This concept of purity is therefore not one in which two people seek to love each other in spirit and truth *in spite* of their bodies, but on the contrary use all the resources of body, mind, heart, imagination, emotion and will in order to celebrate the love that has been given them by God and in so doing to praise Him!

Thomas Merton

EUCHARIST

Anyone who sets out to define the Eucharist might as well try to set precise limits to a cosmic explosion. For what happens in the Eucharist is an event by which our self-enclosed universe is explosively broken open from its innermost center. A chain reaction has been sparked and has released a transforming dynamism which defies limit.

By conceiving the Eucharist as an explosive event, we are able to find the inner connection between its two major aspects. The Eucharist is thanksgiving; and the Eucharist is sacrifice. And once we have perceived how thanksgiving is connected with sacrifice we have gained access to the point from which radiates the relevance of the Eucharist for human life in its totality. We shall briefly attempt to sketch this approach.

A man falls in love, and with one blow the shell of his self-sufficiency is shattered. "Give me a lover," says St.

Augustine, "and he will know what I mean." Your whole life culminates in desire for the one thing which you can never acquire by your own effort: love freely given to you by another. It cannot be forced with a fist; it must be received as a gift into open hands. Nor would love want it any other way. Even in the pangs of unrequited love, the lover still affirms with his whole being the freedom of the beloved.

To the extent to which I do surrender and open myself gratefully to love I begin to live with a new aliveness. But now I come up against death. Love means life. And yet I know that I cannot escape death. Through love I have somehow a share in indestructible life (to love is to know this), and yet I must die. In fact, I am dying at every turn, as my indomitable desire for the infinite paces behind the bars of limitation after limitation like a wild animal kept captive. The more I am alive, the more I am alive to the reality of death—death, not as a point at the end of life, but as the very condition of life as I know it.

I am confronted again with a choice between the two attitudes: fist or open hand. I can clench what I hold and close my eyes to death until its blow falls. I can open hands and eyes, face death and try to discover its meaning. The heart open in confidence asks: "Could the meaning of death be the continuation and completion of that breaking open which love began in me?" Surrendering to love in gratitude, I discovered a fullness of life which my little self, closed in upon itself, could never have suspected, much less contained. And now I have an inkling that surrendering to death in confidence I shall discover a fullness of life which this whole world, closed in upon itself, could neither suspect nor hold. The double blow of death and love liberates my heart (that center of my life where I am most truly myself) by breaking it open for what lies beyond the horizon—beyond the narrow horizon of my individual existence, and beyond the vast horizon of this universe embedded in Mystery.

It is in myth that man's experience of his heart's openness toward the Ultimate first crystallized into poetic images. Two predominant sets of images constantly recurring in primitive myth are grouped around the two ideas of Center and Beginning. Not unlike the child, primitive man is preoccupied with the beginning of things, of man, of the world, because beginning is the "open end" of everything that exists in time. And what beginning means in terms of time, the center symbolizes in terms of space. The navel of man, the Navel of the World, the central support of the tent, the Cosmic Tree—in a multitude of images the center is conceived as the point where the world is open toward the Mystery that lies beyond.

Why is this so? Because man becomes aware that he reaches the center of the universe whenever he returns to his own inmost heart. At the core of his own being he encounters the same Mystery that surrounds his farthest horizon. This intuition of the paradoxical identity between Center and Horizon makes man aware that he himself is destined to be the Cosmic Tree planted in the center of the world, rooted in the depths of the earth, and reaching out into the limitless. And so the Center, standing for man's heart, is conceived as the node of communication with Mystery.

Ritual translates the epic images of myth into dramatic action. Through sacred rites primitive man journeys symbolically to the Center, makes the Beginning present again, and so communicates with Mystery. This is particularly clear in the ritual celebrations which accompany birth, death and the various transitions from one phase of life to another. Each one of these transitions marks the breaking open of one self-contained system of relationships, widens the horizon and gives access to greater fullness of life. These Rites of Passage are meant to channel the power of the Beginning into each new beginning. Sacrifice in one form or other is essential to these rites.

Sacrifice is, in fact, the Rite of Passage. The basic structure of the sacrificial act expresses a passage. Through some symbolic action the sacrificial gift is made to pass from the realm of profane use into the realm of the sacred. Not only the gift, however; the man, too, who offers the gift participates in this passage. In the sacred rite he is identified with the offering; he therefore participates in the transfer that takes place when the gift is offered up, and can communicate with the sacred reality through his share in the consecrated gift. Externally this passage is expressed in the three phases of the sacrificial act: offering (setting aside of the gift), consecration (transfer of the gift) and communion (sharing in the consecrated gift). And though these three phases are not always fully developed in a given example, they are at least germinally present in any form of sacrifice.

If the ritual of sacrifice is thus an expression of man's "passage to the open center," the inner experience which gives rise to this ritual and accompanies it is also one of passage. Its starting point is man in isolation, the goal of its movement is communion. Sacrifice is always a community affair. Communion between man and man, man and the universe, cannot be separated from man's communion with Mystery. The decisive transition from alienation to (ultimately cosmic) integration lies in that same inner gesture of opening hands which we experienced in the liberating acceptance of death and of love.

Openness for the utter mystery that confronts me in death is total openness. And this total openness in the face of death becomes total openness for life. For silhouetted against meaningless death, life becomes meaningful. Seeing life against the background of death, I recognize it as gift. And acknowledging this gift in joyful gratitude, the thankful man integrates death constructively into every moment of life, thus overcoming it without denying it or robbing it of its force. Thanksgiving transforms death into life. Grateful openness of heart makes room in the midst of time for the Great Life that is beyond time. It is this life we mean—not "afterlife" but life in "the now which does not pass away."

The violence often found in sacrificial rites expresses symbolically the high cost of breaking open man's uncommunicative self for life-giving communion with Mystery. My selfish self must die before my true self can find Life. Long before he can express it reflectively, man realizes that to be man is to be open. This is the calling of his heart: to be the open center of the whole world. This is what all things seem to expect from him: to be their eye, their ear, their mouth, their open heart. Yet the realization of this calling is only a hope. Whenever he tries to rise to this challenge, man falls back. His only openness is hope. In leaping and falling he gets to know himself as tentative man, but he does catch glimpses of man as unconditionally open. And in hope he conceives the staggering possibility that his own little self may become one with Man, the definitive man.

And the Gospel is that this Man has come. The whole of our Christian faith is summed up in this proclamation. Man's hope has been fulfilled. If the Incarnation is not a divine afterthought, if man has been created in the image and likeness of God (and the image of the invisible God is Christ), then every true insight man gained into the mystery of his own existence was a glimpse of the Mystery of Christ. No wonder that the historical reality of Jesus Christ should resemble myth. He is the original pattern, and the hero of the myth is merely a tracing of this pattern. We have encountered Him, and we have faith in His claim that it is He.

Professing that this man Jesus is the image of the invisible God, we profess that He is the definitive man. If man is the creature open toward Mystery, and Mystery is the invisible God, the altogether Other beyond the brink of the ultimate horizon, and if we believe in this man who says: "Philip, he who sees Me sees the Father," we believe that in Him unconditional openness has been definitively realized. If then this man takes His whole life and death together in one solemn Rite of Passage, this sacrifice posits in reality what all sacrifices symbolize: access to the Center. This Center is now forever accessible and open: the Heart of Man, opened by a lance.

What does this mean for a Christian? It means that the Eucharist is not an element in Christian life, albeit the most important element. Our life is Christian only to the extent to which it is thanksgiving, Eucharist. And what does this mean for the world? It means that Christians have no monopoly on Eucharistic life. Anything whatsoever, which any man at any time and place takes up into the thanksgiving of his heart, enters into Christ's cosmic Eucharist. The journey to the Center is still a passage through death, but the way is open, irrevocably. An irreversible transformation has been set in motion, a transformation of this universe through thanksgiving—sacrifice. "It has not yet appeared what we shall be." (I John 3:2) But we know that in the end Life, Love, God will be "all in all."

JOY (A POSTSCRIPT)

If we can accept the above, we shall understand why the Liturgy consistently speaks of joy as the fruit of *devotio*. What does this term mean? It is a term charged with the insight of myth and the experience of ritual which we have tried to trace. It means precisely the attitude of one who enters into sacrifice, who sets out on the Dark Journey, the passage through death into life. Joy is not a trimming added to life. Joy is life itself experienced from within. The measure of your joy is the infallible index of the degree to which you are alive. Where there is life there is joy. Where there is true joy, there is true life, life in the openness of thanksgiving, Eucharistic life. Isn't it alarming to think of our churches in this context?

David Rast

World

Every signal of the body and the mind declares with sharp insistency how near and un-out-there it is, how strange the end that blessed ships from Portugal and Spain began to limn one half a thousand years ago. All the tangled (strangled?) cords of need and hope seem ever urging us —against our will how long?—into some uncommon pasture of the gods to find our common ground. Odd, costly piercings of the night at fiery starlike speeds send out new lines for pulling all the mysteries past darkness into light, while children's faces from the farthest streets become our dreams tonight. From infinite space now subject—so we think—to all our super-finitude, from fathoms deeper than our hope, from distances made over into airline stops, from scopes and tubes and from a thousand cables of our heart come all the frantic and staccato jerkings of our shattered wholeness longing for its peace.

But there is a world within each center of these jagged lives that pushes out, forever out, into the stiffened arms of brothers we deny and fast beyond their awkward grasp we speed into the orbits of our own desires, till snatched by forces from the demon air we dance like splintered galaxies toward some new and fiercely burning death.

Meanwhile the white-robed charters of the chartless shout their warnings full across our track, "Do not hope; there is no Master of the spheres, save death."

Was it for this that we left Lisbon, for this that we were stolen from Kilwa, for this that holy fathers poured their holy streams upon our ships? If there is more than questions in the burned-out dark, then let the real Master speak—now—or forever keep his cool.

Vincent Harding

NEGRO

Sign of amnesia in a strange land, symbol of all we have forgotten under the menace of death, the fear of homelessness, the fact of namelessness. Meaning Black—hard, strong, fierce Black—in other tongues; meaning only the property, the slaves, the wards, the clowns in this sad, twisted, frightened tongue. And we (black we) cooperate in loss of our own memory, in denial of our own blackness, in flight from that lost land where long-past fathers rest in pain.

The word marks us like blind amnesiacs as we hear the message of our bondage to the night: "Negro means you have no language but ours. Negro means you have no religion but ours. Negro means (yes, Lord) you have no freedom save that which we deem safe to give. Negro means (my Lord!) you have no dreams except the ragged ones that yet remain from all our dull and whitened blindnesses of night. Negro means—and we alone define—means you love no one but us, and fondle our scorn in the black blankness of your being. Negro, Negro, Nigger, Negro means, ever means (well, Lord!) black Africa is yours only to forget, deny and leave, forever leave. Nigger, Negro means curse now that borning land, its mountains all invisible, its broad grasslands and deserts lost in shadows of your minds."

(And I, black I, take up the song, singing similar but not the same lines.) Negro, not African, not black, means break with traders' whip all families once knit fast for long millennia. Means auction block and cry, baby, cry. Means neither black nor white but Negro, invention of this Christian land, chameleon of this Christian mind. Means fight white wars against enemies declared by whites to remain blank and blind in white men's hands.

Negro, Negro, Negro, pounding out, dashing out each tender intimation of those days when we were Ibo and Yoruba, Ashanti and Kikuyu, denying our beginnings in Mali and Kilwa and on Ife's golden shore. No longer African, veil pulled strangle-tight over the gaspings of our mind. No longer African, refusing nonwhite hands from other lands. No longer African, but never American by dawn's early light; only frantic Negro drifter on white sand. Build your castles and see them fall. Lie down in white darkness and contemplate the blackness of sin, the blackness of dirt, the black, black, blackness of the nigger fear. Lord, Lord, Lord!

Dream. Now dream. Dream seething dreams of your black life beyond this dream when memories shall return. Dream sanity. Dream wholeness. Dream fathers, our fathers. Dream names and tribes and nations and home beyond home. Dream wildly madly of that black black life when "Negro" shall be trampled into every pale and trembling ground and Black men of tribes beyond number shall rise; rise free, dancing free, shouting free, loving free, drumming the message of freedom to the dead amnesiacs called Negroes (and whites?). Dream on to the thunders of your God songs, dream on to the snapping of your devil blues, until there is One to deliver you, or damn you, damn you to live forever as Negro in the quick white sand of the free. My Lord! Who shall deliver us from this body of Negro death?

Vincent Harding

CULTURE

Culture is a Midas' touch that turns everything men do into delight for anthropologists. It is what, seven centuries from now, writers of dreadful texts will instruct college freshmen that we meant, even if now we don't know what we mean. To paraphrase T. S. Eliot, it includes all the characteristic activities and interests of a people: the Superbowl, World Series, Miss America, the Fourth of July, motherhood, anti-communism, chrome door handles, cloverleaves, bank buildings, a Boeing 707, cardboard hamburgers with standardized catsup, folk songs, Cardinal Spellman, the superiority of the white race, and French-fried potatoes. Culture is a cornucopia people living in it cannot make head or tail of.

Culture, in short, is to philosophy as existence is to essence. It is the concrete expression of values too pervasive to be expressed only in words, except centuries later in academic circles.

In a derivative sense, culture is what the rich and the new-rich try to fill their lives with when sexuality falls short. As for the poor (usually referred to as a "subculture"), it is to be said of them, in the words of Camus, "they fornicated and they read the papers."

Michael Novak

CULTURE AND CIVILIZATION

Since Eliot published his *Some Notes towards a Definition of Culture* in 1948, it is with hesitation that anyone hazards a firm definition of that word. It acquired certain sociological connotations during the late nineteenth and early twentieth centuries, for two reasons. First, it came to be used in opposition to the word "civilization" when that word took on a meaning different from the one originally associated with it in the eighteenth century. (It was introduced to describe among the Europeans what was then believed to be a higher level of human conduct than had ever existed before in human societies.) The word "civilization" has since been identified by the cycle historians with a number of different societies, such as the Egyptian, the Persian, the ancient Greek and Roman, the Islamic or the ancient Chinese. For Spengler, who developed the cycle theory to an extreme, culture was the phase in the cycle preceding civilization, the time when the arts flourished. Again, the word "culture" was identified by the Germanic peoples with their own achievements, which were called *Kultur,* the implication being that culture was a kind of preserve of the Germans.

Both these definitions are now, or at any rate should be, abandoned in the light both of history and of common sense. But what should be substituted?

"Culture" has since been annexed by anthropologists, who apply it to any system of manners, customs and laws practiced by a group of humans, whether their society be primitive or civilized. Etienne Gilson has treated culture in this sense as a meaningless word. You must cultivate *something,* he has said. There is the cultivation of the potato, the cultivation of virtue and many other such cultivations: There is no such thing as culture without reference to something specific, he has suggested.

Culture, as Eliot conceived it, and civilization, in the original meaning of that word, are close to one another. Indeed, I am disposed to regard the meaning given to civilization by the Comte de Mirabeau in the eighteenth century as now a valid definition of culture. This is how he defined it: "The civilization of a people is to be found in the softening of manners, in growing urbanity, in politer relations and in the spreading of knowledge in such ways that decency and seemliness are practiced until they transcend specific and detailed laws. . . . Civilization does nothing for society unless it is able to give form and substance to virtue. The concept of humanity is born in the bosom of societies softened by all these ingredients." Civilization in this sense is what people everywhere supremely need in this age when our planet has become a single interdependent entity.

John Nef

POET

Ella ha perduto la sua Beatrice
E le parole ch'uom di lei può dire
Hanno virtù di far piangere altui.

In these childishly simple, strangely moving words Dante has expressed one of the mysteries of the poet: his words have the power to make others weep. He can also make them laugh or smile, but rarely. There were not many Heines in the thirty centuries of poetry, and Heine smiled only "with the laughing tear in the eye." The true power of the poet is plucking at the heartstrings, and making music with them.

Have we still use for such magicians in the technological society of the twentieth century? Are there still people who read poetry because they like a good cry? We have gone far from the eighteenth century when crying at poetry readings was fashionable. Not so long ago we had among us a great revenant of the eighteenth century: Winston Churchill. I remember him making an election speech in 1945 for a candidate whom he had last met at El Alamein. At the words "El Alamein" his voice faltered, he fell silent. One could see in his face the emotions which surged up in him at the memory of the long victorious road along which he had led us since that first great battle, and tears started pouring down his rosy cheeks. But the twentieth-century English audience did not go with him, they cast down their eyes at the painful spectacle of seeing a man weep, and I heard the man next to me murmur, "An old woman!"

The poet is in danger, but so is our whole civilization. By performing his feats of magic, the scientist and the technologist have taken almost all magic out of our lives. Dylan Thomas could, and still can, make people weep, and Edith Sitwell could write beautiful *adagios*, but the attitude of most poets who were born into our century is not serenity: it is cold anger and disgust with our epoch, which they see as a despicable chaos. Aldous Huxley wrote in 1932, between the two world wars: "Would even Dante's abilities suffice to inform our vast and swiftly changing chaos, to build it up into a harmonious composition, to impose a style?" What was true in 1932 is a hundred times more true today. Perhaps there is a hidden harmony beneath the affluent ugliness of our times, perhaps we are on the way to a really Great Society in which there will be no more poverty, squalor and violence, in which the material appetites of men will be sufficiently satisfied to take the edge off their aggressiveness, and which will not drown in cloyed boredom. Perhaps man's spiritual powers are not dead but only hidden beneath a crust of practical cynicism, perhaps those who now write advertising copy because they have the gift of words will start singing of the eternal mysteries of life. But unless great poets will show us the way, it is more than likely that the rich, comfortable material civilization of the next fifty years will breed nothing but angry frustration, which is almost certain to break out in some sort of irrational catastrophe.

Dennis Gabor

LITERATURE

There is a pejorative sense to "literature" as something other than poetry or something which poetry becomes by a process of devitalization. We think of it as having to do with piles of books rather than individual poems—*et tout le reste est littérature.*

When we read "*La chair est triste, hélas! et j'ai lu tous les livres,*" we are likely to feel that if the poet had not read so many books he would not have produced the "literature" of the first hemistich, he would not have thought of his sorrow so grandiosely, or been as content with the gesture of "*La chair est triste*" that he would have let "*hélas*" freeze it and display it for our attention. We may compare "My heart aches and a drowsy numbness pains. . . ." "My heart aches, *hélas*" would be literature, but Keats opens his attention toward other impulses which save and enliven "my heart aches." He has read many of the books, too, and they are present in Proserpine and Lethe, and indeed they threaten to act on him in a numbing way, but even by registering this danger, he frees his literature for poetry.

We can be all too comfortable with this notion of "literature"; it makes us feel superior. But the word carries a sense of genuine pathos, too, which may account for our readiness to patronize it. Because, finally, we *do* love literature—as distinct from poetry, essay, novel or whatever, and we love it out of a weakness that does much to explain the strength of poetry. The love of literature, as Mallarmé saw, has its origins in the sorrows of the flesh, though it cannot satisfy them. And poetry, which can never separate itself from literature, returns us to the joy of the flesh—to ourselves—by going beyond literature. The poet becomes "*Tel qu'en Lui-meme l'Éternité le change,*" which may at first seem to be the stodgiest of "literary" formulae, but in fact is not. Poetry never turns out to be what we expect from literature, but it builds upon those expectations.

Augustine comes to mind as the type of the man *interested in literature,* the reader with revolutionary expectations, who looks to a book for an event that will determine his history. Though it is scripture that he finally takes and reads, at the moment of his final revelation he is not treating it as scripture; he concentrates, not on the writer, but on the letter (*litera*) itself. In other words, he is concentrating on the object read, on the book, as the relieving and transforming agency, the immediate source of a new order in his life. Our emotions toward books, the sense of possibility, hope and reverence which we invest in the word literature, the elation and dizziness we experience in bookstores—as if in contact with the very body of *Kultur*

—clearly reflect this desire for revolutionary transformation. The impulse is richly caught by James in *The Ambassadors,* when all Strether's intuitions of the revival of a buried life that Paris seems to promise are embodied in the bright yellow books he sees on the stalls, "lemon-colored volumes as fresh as fruit on the tree." For Strether, literature is books, not poems or arguments or authors. It stands for the entire range of unreleased gestures, visions, capabilities that the fullness of his body seems, at least in retrospect, to have held out to him. Like Augustine, confused and baffled by years of high education and undischarged desires, far from home, longing for clarity at a time of crisis, he feels that literature itself, books, a book, any book, taken and read, may hold the key.

This appetite for literature most commonly takes the form of some kind of connoisseurship, which—as the connoisseur's favorite metaphor of "taste" suggests—is a substitute gratification, love for books as consumable, touchable, "tastable" objects. But however deflected, the appetite is ultimately an appetite for life, and the connoisseur, like Augustine, may be converted by what he reads—though not to a dogma. A successful poem transforms its consumer by refusing to be an object. The glittering book dissolves and leaves us surprised, turned loose on the world. Poetry disguises itself as literature in order to free itself for life.

Michael Goldman

BEAUTY

Contemporary artists and writers are guided, it would seem, by the powerful feeling that whatever beauty is, it should be come by not directly but indirectly. There is a paradox here that seems to be a determinant of taste and method. The paradox is that beauty is indeed to be sought and reached, but not by way of beauty.

If you aim directly at beauty, the thought is, you may very well emerge with a well-made, well-ordered thing, but also a thing touched by superficiality or irrelevance. But if, taking our example from tragic literature, you simply aim at the unfathomably sad story of a broken man, you may very well come up with beauty, but not, obviously, by way of beauty. For who would say that tragedy, or the human at its most exhausted, could be beautiful? It is as though there is some hidden dictum in much art that only by giving up beauty will you find it: He who loses his soul will find it. For what, according to any direct theory of or search for beauty, can be beautiful about Oedipus, Cassandra, Prometheus, Hecuba, Macbeth, Lear, Othello, and a long history of others broken on the wheel of life? This must be remembered when we read a good deal of the modern novel or writing for the theater, or look at a great picture like Picasso's "Guernica." The aim is at the human, at its best and worst. Very often what is being looked at is the incomparable loneliness of men and women, and this is a frequent subject of the greatest film artists and directors of our day. But there is nothing directly or immediately beautiful about loneliness, or desperation, or destruction.

What is true of tragedy is even more true of the comic. For there we often have man at his most actual, far from any ideal we so often talk about as beauty. In comedy, man is sometimes fat, sometimes stupid, sometimes confused, but never beautiful. Yet, it often turns out beautifully. We pick up the text of Shakespeare's *Henry IV* and we follow the full, fat outlines of Falstaff and might wonder what is beautiful or "artistic" about such a reality. Or we turn to the contemporary play *Mother Courage* by Bertolt Brecht, and we hear this mighty lady defend the small and not necessarily the great or beautiful ones of our earth:

> I feel sorry for a commander or an emperor like that —when maybe he had something special in mind, something they'd talk about in times to come, something they'd raise a statue to him for. The conquest of the world now, *that's* a goal for a commander, he couldn't do better than *that,* could he? . . . Lord, worms have got into the biscuit . . . in short he works his hands to the bone and then it's all spoiled by the common

riffraff that only wants a jug of beer or a bit of company, not the higher things in life. The finest plans have always been spoiled by the littleness of them that should carry them out. Even emperors can't do it by themselves. They count on support from their soldiers and the people round about. Am I right?

I, for one, think she is right. I think the Emperor called Beauty comes from smaller, more indirect things than the emperor called beauty.

William Lynch

JUSTICE

Justice is to make action conform to reality, the most difficult and noble of enterprises. Law is one of its instruments and, like politics, a method for institutionalizing the practice of justice, institutionalizing our reconciliation of Eros and Thanatos. Justice is a preposterous and unfulfillable ambition since reality is as unknowable as God, perceived only as in a thousand pieces of shattered reflection, and human action is perverse. But thus do we sustain ourselves against the dissolution and isolation that draw us so powerfully. Justice is possible only if we have reconciled ourselves to the fact of its impossibility.

William Pfaff

LAW

Shall we ever break the diamond-bright and hardened shackles, loose the condemning bands of death between this precious word and those other citadels of brittle sanity: "and order" (God, what blasphemy against the spirit's freedom flight), "and order"?

With the first word come announcements of new hope, creation of an atmosphere where souls may meet and steal into the deep and tender power of a cataclysmic birth of joy. Law stands positive and gentle-strong as loving source of our best peace, as climate of the mind set free from all the chains of snarling narcissistic night.

Insistent upon the justice for which broken spirits long, demanding rights for speechless lives which grasping power would so lawfully deny, searching out those worlds where weak and trusting gentle power fears no lion in the gate, where no hate-bred fury will destroy the gutted spirits of the crushed and beaten men. Law brings the gospel to the Church's fallen victims and celebrates the justice of its long-forgotten Lord. (While Church cries out that law is not enough, that love must yet prevail, but stands unceasingly apart from even one first lawful step toward love.) Such law is free translation of all those best and swinging dreams men dare release from nights of painful love.

But joy is always prey to calculated brutal strength, and law is set upon with endless din by "order," always "order," posing as a friend but weaving webs of death around its feet and pulling out its tongue and setting systems of the victors' sounds into the frozen lips of death. Now law is the deadly mocking smile at all the hopes of vanquished men, and in its lifeless form it moves at power's whim and stands against the doors to freedom's land, and arms police against the ghetto's dying, borning band. Such law laughs cynics' tears at revolutions all disemboweled by the cruel, cutting fingers of a search long past into the night of grim despair. Lost, transformed, cocoon-enwrapped by steel, like the mummy of the world's most gracious queen, law stands, a prop for death. Now with its future long and oh so sadly past, there seems to live no one last hope—except, perhaps, that death-clothed mimic of a life once born shall be by men (indignant, holy, dispossessed and dying men) thrown down and broken into dust again. Then, if he comes, a new God may begin afresh.

Vincent Harding

SCIENCE

Science has reached a new threshold of meaning. The shifts toward system and explanation began when the ancient civilizations and Renaissance city-states had occasioned new pressures and risks through the maze of their activities on the spontaneous level of meaning. In analogous fashion, the uncontrolled yet phenomenal expansion in the explanatory mediation of the natural sciences is demanding a new shift in, and enlargement of, the scientist's intellectual horizon. Nor are indications lacking of the direction the shift is taking. On practically every side the human subject is intruding into science and science into history.

There is a difference between the meaning of a natural event and a human, historical event. Man did not create the material universe with its multiple physical, chemical, biological and psychological processes. But men do make history. We cannot avoid the action or inaction that shapes our personal, community, national and world histories. We're all on the stage, and no matter what we do or fail to do, it is part of the play. Thus, the meaning of nature has always been a mediated one, it comes to us either through the descriptive symbols of the world of community or the explanatory understanding of the world of theory. On the other hand, human events are not only mediated by meaning, they are constituted by it. We may think the play, or at least our role, is absurd and meaningless—then that is the meaning we give it. Pessimists make history no less than optimists.

The sciences have been making history too, but in an unguided and unscientific way. For science is the mediation of explanatory understanding, and while the latter has been busy investigating the secrets of nature it has not come to grips with its own, or any other, constitutive meaning. Human actions are the stuff of history, an explanation of one cannot get along without that of the other. Hence the contemporary stage in the scientific revolution must shift toward the subject, toward human interiority. The depth psychology of Freud and Jung was a good inauguration. Enormous work remains to be done. By and large the human sciences have been too preoccupied with the methods of the physical sciences to recognize how the new dimension of meaning they are dealing with cannot be handled adequately by natural categories.

Ironically, the natural sciences themselves are being forced to make their history scientific. Heisenberg has introduced the subject into nuclear physics. Meanwhile pure and applied science are found to be reverse sides of the same coin, and their power to recreate the world of matter and man is too vast for scientists to securely adopt a *laissez-faire* policy. They are giving us the ability to fashion new elements, synthesize new chemicals, direct biological evolution, control psychological development, manage public opinion, project industrial society out of work through cybernetics.

In a word, science is allowing history to engulf more and more of nature—and history has not yet been understood scientifically. (What is called scientific history is still in the descriptive stage of system, it describes and classifies rather than explains what happened.) The risks are too great to permit haphazard applications by unconsciously biased minds. If science's nerve fails now, everything will probably be lost. It has to push on to explain the inner world of the subject. Only then will the human sciences forge methods intelligent enough to explain the meaning of man and his history, and critical enough to sharply distinguish between progress and decline. The human scientist has to master the social surd with a success comparable to the mathematician's and physicist's mastering of theirs.

The first half of our century saw man's relation to the rest of nature explored; now scientists find themselves grappling with the meaning proper to man. As the probing advances, science may discover how closely related it is to wisdom. The Greeks have priceless lessons to teach us about the human spirit—we dare not shy away just because our modernity is embarrassed to sit next to an alert medieval friar. The shift toward the subject should lead to an explication and appropriation of the intelligent and rational dynamisms through which the sciences were born and grew. A correlating of the ever-increasing specialized sciences by means of such inner dynamics would effect an organic order that at the same time would be open to all future developments.

It would also relate science to the rest of man's life. The two-culture problem is very much a sign of our times.

It results from the accelerated differentiation in mental horizons between the worlds of community and of theory. Literary creativity encounters the mystery of man in all of its depth and unpredictable freedom. To convey this fullness, art struggles to incarnate its insight in the descriptive symbols that speak to more than the intellect. Science, too, is concerned with mystery, but to explain it, to confront precisely limited aspects of it in the hope of understanding. A day will never dawn when men will raise no further questions. Science will never explain all the mystery intimated in art.

Scientists do not live exclusively in laboratories, nor are artists always in ecstasy. The new shift of science toward the human subject should clarify where an authentic integration of the two cultures has to occur. Only when aware of our own inner activities in moving back and forth between the world of community and the world of theory will we, as intelligent citizens of both, be capable of integrating in our own lives the irreplaceable values of each. It is bad art and worse science to see solutions to cultural alienation in computers ejecting odorless, automatic verse, or in people who try to squeeze poetry out of logarithms.

Science has come a long way since the first opening to system and the second to explanation. If the uncertainty of crisis or glory haunts its third challenge, neither better equipment nor larger congresses are going to decide the issue. Scientists will have to take seriously the Socratic injunction to know oneself, so seriously that they come up with answers Socrates never knew. A terrible global hemlock may be the only alternative.

Matthew Lamb

World

The world, by contrast to the nation, is scary in scale, a community we recognize but where our relationships are not felt. There is no patriotism possible here. There is little knowledge, and modern communications have given the material means for knowledge but the illusion of understanding. By technology we are far more able to hurt one another, and more likely because our fear of strangers and the vulnerability of our isolation are given material warrant. Our intuition of a common fate creates in us a panicked concern at the hostility of others. We want to control the harm others can do; we are frightened; we want to disarm this threat by making others believe and live as we do. We call this helping them, or saving them, but it is an act of sublimated fear.

In the past the remoteness which technology has broken down provided protection. The modern interac-

tion and communication of societies is creative, but it is also destructive. The self-confidence and self-respect of the old civilizations of Asia have been crucially undermined by this encounter. The primitive cultures of Africa have been shattered. In succession, Europe, Russia and the United States have aggressively asserted standards of values and conduct for the world, and have attempted to enforce these. Imperialism often has been meanly inspired by arrogance and a desire for power and exploitation. But its ultimate horror, for Asians and Africans, has been that the intellectual and moral power of the imperialists has been as great as their material power. Their brilliance has equaled their capacity for power and crime. Their values have been asserted with the intolerant zeal that the universalism of Western intellectual tradition inspires—and those values have not conquered; they have willingly been seized. The West is Faust; the rest of the world has been recruited to Faustianism. This is the meaning of the contemporary world political revolution.

William Pfaff

NATION

The nation is a self-defined human community, necessary because of what Jaspers has called "the bottomlessness of the world," the threat of the condition of nihilism. The source of the word is *natio,* "birth," the nation as being the offspring of a common birth, a clan. It is a provisional reconciliation of the human impulses to unity and to isolation. It enables men to relate their lives to the lives of others.

The contemporary nation is a community of manageable and emotionally intelligible scale. If it is provisional, transitional, we do not know what it is in transition to. Where a transition appears to be taking place, as in contemporary Western Europe, the successor-community, in this case "Europe," already exists but has acquired a new power over the loyalties and self-identification of its members by becoming, emotionally, reduced in scale. It has been placed under competitive challenge by extra-European communities. Yet what here is spoken of as "Europe" is, of course, no more than Europe's Atlantic edge. Central and northern Europe, Iberia, the Balkans, are all excluded, yet they are crucially implicated in the European historical experience. And the success of even this Western European transition in political community is by no means assured. The power over men of the myth of nation remains very great; where, in transition, does unity end and dissolution, isolation, begin? In much of the world beyond the West the perceived community, the felt relationship, the solidarity, remains smaller in scale than the official nation.

John Nef

PATRIOTISM

Patriotism articulates a community, usually by bad poetry and intolerantly, fictionalizing the virtues of the community and inventing reasons to reinforce its power over us and reassure us in our fears of isolation. It is the rationalized expression of something which has nonrational but true sources.

William Pfaff

FATHERLAND

The origin of this word as a designation for one's country seems obscure. But in the late nineteenth and early twentieth centuries the word came to be associated widely with the German-speaking countries, with Germany in particular, partly no doubt because of its use in a German national anthem. On account of this association and the violent connotation later given to the word by the Nazi dictatorship, fatherland expresses nationalism in its extreme form. It contains the connotation of the nation above all, of "our country right or wrong."

The word, therefore, is peculiarly inappropriate to the new conditions under which we find ourselves since the coming of nuclear weapons and the complete technological interdependence of all parts of this planet. In the new context, fatherland is a word which we should associate only with God the Father, on the understanding that this association can never be exclusive but must always be comprehensive, that it must be based on love of the neighbor and on the conviction that all men are brothers and sisters. Since the new weapons man has devised would be safe only in the hands of a deity whose principle is love, the revolution in human conditions which many of us have witnessed in our lifetime makes it imperative that the word be redefined in this most comprehensive and gentle sense.

John Nef

SOVEREIGNTY

Sovereignty is how and by whom the toughest decisions are finally settled. It has the last word, and the power to enforce. Lacking sovereignty, you have anarchy, although there are, or have been, quite a number of amiable mixtures of the two. But in times of crisis, that is, when the decisions get tough, these blends separate out, and either sovereignty is established or anarchy is. That is why most anarchists, when forced to explain how their system, or non-system, can endure, tend to insist on the fact of abundance: Once having removed the present distortions in either man's ability to produce or his desire to consume, there will be plenty, no, more than plenty, to go around. Thus, no tough decisions.

Among and between sovereignties there is anarchy. As long as nation-states are sovereign, international relations are essentially anarchical. This fact has led sensitive men, and even Dean Rusk, to occasionally denounce sovereignty as outdated. Of course, such men are frequently citizens of areas where sovereignty has long been a settled matter—while in a great part of the world it still remains unsettled; and the conflicting claims of kin, tribe, caste, race, and nation, in the absence of a sovereign to judge between them, hamstring the making of crucial decisions. The shift from anarchy to a system of sovereignty is a tremendously difficult one. It has never been accomplished without violence. A century of Western philosophers from Hobbes to Rousseau used the terms "state of nature" and "social contract" to analyze just what this shift meant, for good or evil, and how it could be justified.

These philosophers approached the problem from the point of view of rational man. More recently, Freud described the social contract in terms of irrational man: It was formed by the bond of guilt, the guilt of the sons who have murdered the father of the primal horde. The theory casts an interesting light on the establishment of the League of Nations and the United Nations—half-hearted attempts at new social contracts—after the two world wars. The magic took only to the extent that the guilt lasted.

Neither worldwide misery nor worldwide warfare can be avoided unless we have new sovereignties. We need effective national social contracts and eventually we need a world social contract, and these two needs, to a large extent, conflict. The problem is perplexing; the Freudian shadow cannot be banished. Will it take our guilt over global catastrophes, whether famine or war, to give birth to new social contracts?

Peter Steinfels

CAPITALISM

Capitalism is a word frequently associated with Karl Marx. But, so far as I have been able to discover, Marx never actually used the word, although he wrote a great deal about capital, and, indeed, used it as the title for the most massive of his books. Since Marx's time the word came to be identified, in the language first of economists and then of economic historians, with what was thought to be a particular, and more or less novel, system of production.

This was a system under which the means of production—industrial plant and tools, raw materials and partly finished products of all kinds in process of manufacture—were owned by private persons. These persons were frequently called capitalists. According to the definition which was fairly widespread, capitalists hire laborers in a free market and pay them wages which are fixed, in the language of economists, by the laws of supply and demand.

A great deal of inquiry was done by students of history into the origins of capitalism, in this sense of the word. For a time it was supposed that capitalism originated in modern Europe, and flourished especially during and since the eighteenth century, gradually extending to all parts of the world. But students of history later found plenty of examples of capitalistic enterprise in earlier societies, for example, in ancient Greece and in China during the Sung Dynasty of the tenth and eleventh centuries.

Another complicating factor, so far as the original concept of capitalism is concerned, came with the rise of the modern industrialized world. More and more, and not only in Communist countries, private capital came increasingly under the control of the state. By the late twentieth century freedom in the use of capital had become something of a myth even in the most allegedly free-enterprise countries.

The whole concept of capitalism is in need of radical overhaul. What makes the word especially misleading is the widespread identification of the phrase with the affluent economy and population explosion which have come upon the world during the last one hundred and especially the last fifty years. It is wrongly, but very widely, assumed that this affluence is to be explained entirely in economic terms, and that capitalism or anticapitalism was responsible for it.

Actually, history is far less simple. All aspects of man's and woman's activities have played a role in the coming of industrialism, a human condition which economic historians have tended frequently to regard as the result almost exclusively of capitalism. The pursuit of beauty in all realms—from literature to painting and architecture, abstract thought in philosophy and in science—perhaps even more than in economics, has shaped the modern world which staggers us. Therefore, it is only by treating individuals as wholes again, and seeing history as a whole, that the human race might learn to cope with the overwhelming problems produced by industrialism.

John Nef

MARXISM

Not long ago one studied Marxism as one might the enemy code—to crack it. To know the official texts and the obscure disputes was a highly regarded achievement, but for refutation purposes only. To be able to describe the pathetic history of socialist splits—it placed one on a pedestal of wisdom, above the sordid history of our era, above those quarrels simultaneously considered petty and responsible for all ensuing calamities. On a popular level, Bishop Sheen would explain the errors of Marx to everyone not watching *I Love Lucy*. A decade of high school students chuckled to find out that all Karl Marx's prophecies had turned out just as wrong as Mary Baker Eddy's. In 1950, a distinguished American sociologist could declare, "Marxist thought in all its Communist and Social Democratic varieties and its assorted heterodoxies has become a collection of clichés."

No longer. A thoughtful discussion of politics or social change, of philosophy or economics, can hardly begin these days before someone finds it necessary to get a foothold in Marx. What Benedetto Croce recalled about the Italy of the 1890s seems applicable to the United States of the 1960s. Marxism, he wrote, had "won over all, or almost all, the flower of the youth. . . . To remain uninfluenced and indifferent to it, or to assume, as some did, an attitude of unreasoning hostility toward it, was a sure sign of inferiority."

As a matter of fact, brethren, today the pendulum is on the other foot.

A little Marxist seasoning is *de rigueur* among social activists; and Bright Young Graduate Students or even Professors Who Are Not Out of It are tempted to sprinkle their discourses with a little *1844 Manuscripts* or *German Ideology*. Marxism has become a sort of lingua franca of the intellectuals, allowing them not merely to communicate ideas, but, far more important, to swiftly sort one another out according to ideological accents.

Which is not precisely what Marx had in mind. But has Marxism ever been what Marx had in mind? Poor Marx! Overhearing his doctrines explained by his son-in-law, he declared that if that was Marxism he wasn't a Marxist. And any amateur Marxiologist can tell he was terribly misunderstood by his collaborator of forty years, Friedrich Engels.

By now, we have had a positivist Marx, a Darwinian Marx, a Kantian Marx, a Freudian Marx, an existentialist Marx, and most recently a Roman Catholic Marx. Sorel gave us a Nietzschean anarchist version, Lenin a Russian Jacobin one, and Mao Tse-tung. . . . For part of the globe, Marxism is the established church, with its own rituals, popes, catechisms, curias and heretics. From the theory of a postindustrialization, postcapitalist transformation, it has turned into a mainspring of industrialization, filling in for capitalism where the latter has failed the job. These many Marxisms spring partly from unresolved contradictions in Marx's own work; but they also testify to the compelling quality of that work, attracting such a variety of men to put it to their own uses, forcing them to reconcile it with their own circumstances or previous beliefs.

So what, as a well-known Marxist once asked, is to be done?

Make our own Marxism? Of course—though not with an Up-to-Date Marxism Kit (some of these are actually becoming available, disguised as paperback books). Marxism—after all, before all, above all—was what Karl Marx *did,* all his life long. It is not his classical economics or his surplus labor theory of profit or his theory of classes we need to remake; it is the *project* he undertook. Believing in a man radically incomplete yet destined to be radically fulfilled, Marx determines to find out how things *really* work. He criticizes his mentors; learns from his opponents; refuses any convenient but cloudy consensus with those who are vaguely on the same "side." He was dedicated, *effectively,* to revolution; he was dedicated, *effectively,* to truth; and in fact he insisted that the two could not emerge, *effectively,* except together. This two-handed grasp, on revolution and truth, is Marx's greatest challenge to all who come after him. Lesser men have always had to let go with one hand or the other. Even in Marx's case, the struggle took its toll; he became cranky and belligerent; when the strain became too great, he might patch his theory with a polemic. But he held on.

Still, at this project, Marx probably failed. We can say

that now. From the point of view of every century, the one before it failed. But Marx came closer than anyone since. In our time, Sartre has tried (mainly earning disdain for his courage), and *his* failure shows the extent of Marx's success.

So let us try our own *German Ideology* (or *Western Ideology* or *Left Ideology*), our own *Manifesto,* our own *Capital.* Our project is like Marx's: to refuse (a) to be gulled, either by society or our best friends, and (b) to give up.

Postscript: When the constitution of the First International was written in 1864, an incident occurred which has been cherished ever since by the anti-Marxist gossips. A reference to "right and duty, justice and freedom" was inserted, which led Marx to explain to Engels that he had tolerated this only because the words were in a context where "they could do no possible harm." The gesture should not be sneered at. Nor should it be copied, but *followed:* today's words would be different. They might include "free world." Or "foreign aid." Or "people's democracies." Or even "alienation." Karl Marx, troublesome man, might even demand today that a revolutionary organization dedicate itself to "right and duty, truth, justice, and freedom."

Peter Steinfels

REVOLUTIONISTS

Recent history has made China from a politically archaic nation into the most radical in the world. This is no coincidence, of course: in 1917, Tsarist Russia made a similar Big Leap. The longer the men of power in a country hold on to the past, the bigger the splash when they are finally forced to let go.

The Chinese Revolution is only the third social revolution in modern times; our search for parallels and precedents is therefore limited. At this time, the spring of 1967, its course seems to have veered sharply away from the Russian example. The Soviets—no matter what they *said* —quickly settled down to a quite pragmatic policy of "making the best" of their situation, and Soviet foreign policy soon lost all Marxist coloring. China today presents no such spectacle of compromise. It reminds me rather of revolutionary France in the years 1792 and 1793, when the Jacobins were determined not to be satisfied with what had been gained so far, but preached permanent revolution. And they did so partly in spite, but partly because, of an inimical world and their own emigrants, standing armed at the borders. They lost, of course, and when Robespierre and Babeuf had been beheaded, that era was over and done with. Napoleon may have been, in modern terms, an aggressor, but he was not a revolutionary. The similarities with the Chinese situation are obvious, and once more the world hopes (perhaps, once more, ill-advisedly) for a triumph of Girondists over Jacobins.

But underneath and outside of this struggle, Chinese communist society *looks* much more normal to a Western visitor than the ephemeral reporting, and the frenzied demonstrations and denunciations, would lead one to expect. Daily life goes on. The people work thc fields as they have for six thousand years, and they are somewhat better fed and clothed than they used to be. The deep, essential change for them is the "moneylessness" of their world: not its poverty, but the fact that money, as such, plays such a minor role.

Here is a world in which relationships of work, profession and business are not steered by the classical rules of profit and economy; thus, other disciplinary and steering forces are needed to make it function. The sum of these forces make up the New Morality. One: every Chinese must be fed, housed, clothed and educated *because* he is Chinese, and he must be his (Chinese) brother's keeper; and Two: every Chinese must work as well as he can for his country. Propositions One and Two are parallel; Number Two is supposedly not pursued to provide for Number One. This society is noneconomic and vastly experimental —a quality passed over by those who discuss Mao as if he were only a latter-day Kublai Khan.

Perhaps we had something reminiscent of it in the Middle Ages before the rise of early capitalism, when custom and Christianity provided the rules. Perhaps we should not even talk about capitalism versus communism but about a "money society" versus a "rules society." Such a rules society would function best in isolation, and the intense isolation of China, imposed on it by the United States since 1949 and by the U.S.S.R. since 1959, paradoxically creates the right climate for its drastically different character. In this atmosphere, it isn't so strange or unbelievable any more that government tax collectors became incorruptible, that waiters *really* don't want tips, that a lost wallet is always brought back, that doors do not have to be locked, and that some intellectuals want to prove that they no longer feel contempt for peasants by lugging buckets of manure in their free time. The pat answers of people, questioned about their wishes for the future, that they'll do what's best for everyone, become less annoyingly smug and less unreal; it becomes conceivable that at least some of them mean it.

What happens to the voices of dissent in this very particular society? They have no chance; in a sense they are sacrificed. That does not mean that a majority of the population of China is against the revolution. "Why then," asks the visitor, "hasn't China, has no country like China, ever had a real election, which would prove this?"

Paraphrasing many comments on this, the answer of some Chinese politicians would be that "the demands which the revolution makes on the people are too intense to admit the doubt of choice." "If we open the doors, people would go in all directions, and the revolution would perish. Western economy, or democracy, seems to us to be based on the fact that man is bad, totally selfish.

Accepting this, you try to make your society work without appealing to man's morality.

"This is a bleak assumption. We want to think that our people are finally going to be better-than-they-ought-to-be, that they can be made ready for the brotherhood of man; but only if we show them we are totally sure of what we are doing will they accept the discipline. They have to be made to, because they are weak. . . . In Russia, they are drifting back to the old ways . . . We will not let them."

It is precisely on this point that the Chinese power struggle—now open, possibly soon covert only—focuses. It is a struggle *among* Communists this time; the political spectrum of the world has shifted left since 1792! There are those who hold that these principles of discipline and morality are means to an end, means to pull the nation up by its bootstraps. When there is rice on every plate and goldfish in every goldfish bowl, this bleak world is to be abandoned, and "Western" normalcy is to be aimed for. But there are others, who may be called Maoists, for convenience's sake. They, burning with a medieval saintly fervor, consider a more or less bourgeois China as much of a lost cause as a China defeated in war by the United States. They feel there is no salvation but in continuing revolution. To an easily tired world, they present the somewhat uncomfortable spectacle of revolutionaries who do not grow weary.

Hans Koningsberger

THE CROSS

At the center of revolution in our times stands the Cross. Chesterton says, "Though the Cross has at its heart a collision and a contradiction, it can extend its four arms forever without altering its shape. Because it has a paradox at its center, it can grow without changing." It is precisely this changeless growth of essential contradiction that provides us with revolution without end. When the crucifixion took place, no less than now, it was an affirmation of values until then denied, a denial of others until then affirmed. The ends preferred to seeking first the kingdom of God lay defeated. A Messiah creating economic abundance, political supremacy, social prestige for his followers—the image was forever ruined by the disgraced man on the Cross.

In the Cross, for the first time in history, men saw a union of perfect justice and love in response to the sacrifice demanded by the Father. In human ways also, this antinomy was revealed. Beyond justice, the conquered King freed from scorn the victims of greed, prejudice, hate, in a fellowship of love. Men still demand mercy as the crown of justice, not only in the fellowship of Christ crucified, but in a sharing of their condition by His followers. The rights of human dignity can be restored only when charity informs just law.

"He loved me and delivered Himself for me" has long expressed the attitude of the individual before the Cross, but today another more comprehensive saying of St. Paul holds the attention: "It was God's good pleasure to let all completeness dwell in Him, and through Him to win back all things, whether in earth or in heaven, into union with Himself, making peace with them through His blood, shed on the Cross." The modern Christian finds in Christ not only his individual suffering experienced, but the agony of all creation. This includes in a special way his own "civilization," for "wherever the Cross appears, unrest and antagonisms are inevitable. . . . Jesus on the Cross is both the symbol and the reality of the immense labor of the centuries which has little by little raised up the created spirit and brought it back to the depths of the divine context."

The centuries with their labors, however, in witnessing the development of our modern situation, and placing it in the divine context, have not prevented its predicament. Rather, they have brought it to a climax—a climax in which the Cross is still at the center of the antagonisms.

The Cross is not an armchair. By its very stance it repudiates unrealities. Those who preach its meaning today from the defended positions of comfort and withdrawal can only hope to intellectualize its horror, to present to disinterested beholders an unconvincing and pale Galilean. The discreet mildness of the conventional crucifix makes us oblivious to torture, just as the idealized revolution fought merely with letters to the editor has substituted for the sacrificial battle which destroys that it may create. Thomas Jefferson, close enough to a genuine revolution to know suffering, borrowed from the symbol of the crucifix when he said that the Tree of Liberty must be watered from time to time with blood. In this age of anodynes, we question how prepared we are for the kind of revolution the Cross in our times may demand. Only in Christ crucified, with arms extended to Jew and gentile, can these two opposed peoples be reconciled; only in the side of Christ, opened on the Cross, can Negro and white fraternally meet; only in the oneness of a divine and human sacrifice can the conflict of the nations be ended. Although the price of peace has been paid with the tortures of Christ, His merits have not been fully applied.

Sister Mary Immaculate Creek, C.S.C.

DEATH

Life comes into being without any invitation of our own: we suddenly find ourselves in it. And as soon as we recognize ourselves as alive, we become aware that we tend toward inevitable death. If we do not gain some adequate understanding of our life and our death, during the life span that is ours, our life will become nothing but a querulous refusal, a series of complaints that it must end in death. Then the fear of death becomes so powerful that it results in a flat refusal of life. Life itself becomes a negation, a neurosis, a frivolity.

When life and death lose their proper meaning, that is to say, when they are no longer experienced as what they really are, then the awful and empty power of death creeps into everything and sickens everything. So when death becomes most trivial, it also becomes most pervasive. It is only "the end of life." So all life ends. All is death. Why live?

To take death seriously is not, by any means, to seek to avoid it always and at all costs, but to see that it must come as part of a development, as part of a living continuity that has an inner meaning of its own. Death contributes something decisive to the meaning of life. Therefore death does not simply "intervene" or "supervene" and spring upon life as upon its prey, in order to devour it. To hypostatize death—to give it an objective and autonomous reality of its own, a "power" of its own, and set it over against life—does not make death serious but trivial. And yet, this way of thinking does in fact give death a kind of power over life, at least in our own minds. Thus we *live as if* death were always ready to exercise this inescapable power over us. We take to living mouse-lives that are always waiting for the cat, death. Yet there is no cat, and we are not mice. If we do in fact "die," it is not because a monster has caught up with us, and pounced on us at last. If we become obsessed with the idea of death hiding and waiting for us in ambush, we are not making death more real but life less real. Our life is divided against itself. It becomes a tug of war between the love and the fear of life. Death then operates in the midst of life, not as the end of life, but rather as the *fear* of life. Death is life afraid to love and trust itself because it is obsessed with its own contingency and its own ending.

That we inevitably take this wrong attitude toward life and death (we cannot help it) is, according to the Bible, the sign and the effect of sin. Sin and death go together, for when our attitude toward life becomes infected with sin (and every man's attitude is so infected), then life is seen as something that must inevitably be ambushed by death. But when is life seen in such a light? This is the important question, for on this depends our notion of the *end* of life. And when we pause to reconsider this fact, we see that the word "end" is ambiguous. This ambiguity is close to the heart of that ignorance of life (and consequent fear of death) which is, in its turn, such an important element in what we call "sin."

The "*end*": that is to say, the *termination*, the *abrupt and arbitrary conclusion.* The Greeks thought of the thread of life being cut by the scissors of the Fates. Death is then the destruction of something that need not end. The termination of the interminable. This brings us to a better idea of the sinful concept of life: the word *interminable* is quite suggestive. Though there is no real reason why life should simply go on and on and on, we feel that this interminability is nevertheless owed to life. We find that life is therefore an incomprehensible *datum,* something thrust upon us, something that wants to continue, something that, even though meaningless, declares itself, in its inmost strivings and aspirations, to be "interminable." This experience of life, which we are now characterizing as that which is born of sin, is therefore completely ambiguous and, in fact, very distressing. Life is something meaningless that seeks to perpetuate itself without reason and to be simply and arbitrarily interminable. Over against this is death, which is life's enemy, and seeks, always with ultimate success, to terminate it. Two arbitrary forces meet in this unreasonable conflict, and death always wins. Something which for no reason wants to be interminable is in fact terminated. An essentially meaningless life-drive demands to continue in spite of everything, and we choose to adjust our lives to this demand. But the situation itself seems fatally unjust. Therefore we tend, as sinners, to meet it equivocally. We know that death cannot be turned aside by deceit, yet we try to live lives that will at least outwit death as long as possible. The sinful life is one which, for no reason except that we seek to outwit death, becomes a hectic and desperate drive to assert life's own interminability. This compounds all the inner ambiguities of life and death. For one thing, in seeking to convince themselves of their own power to survive, men seek to destroy others who are weaker than themselves. In destroying others, the victors strive to feel themselves interminable, since in the presence of another's suffering and death they themselves go on more lustily than before. They go home and celebrate their new lease on life—which has, however, come from the experience and spectacle of death. In the society of men who are exclusively intent on their own pleasure and survival, even though it has no meaning, just because they are convinced that their life ought to be interminable, death begins to play a very important part. Death is called upon to nourish and to stimulate the "sense of life."

This immediately begets another and far worse ambiguity. A "sense of life" that is habitually fed on death is corrupt and pathological. It is not life at all. In seeking to escape death, man becomes fatally attracted by the death he seeks to escape. His obsession with avoiding death becomes a fascinated and hypnotized flirtation with death. Thus, death in fact comes to be the "end" of life not in the sense of its termination only, but more especially as its *goal.*

Psychoanalysis has taught us something about the death wish that pervades the modern world. We discover our affluent society to be profoundly addicted to the love of death, and most of all when it seems to be carried away by the celebration of life. Erich Fromm has pointed out how obsession with power and wealth inevitably means obsession with death. The death-oriented mind not only directs its energies to obviously destructive uses of power (such as nuclear stockpiling), but even its apparently productive work is in fact a work of death, a work centered on reducing life to "dead things" and depersonalizing men, reducing them to objects, to commodities for use. The love of money is in fact the love of a "dead" product (which is nevertheless endowed with magic life), and we know how psychoanalysis explains this. The anal character is a death-loving character, and he expresses his love of death not only in avarice, in the accumulation of power, but also in legalism (the deadening of life and impulse by the hand of law) and technologism (the substitution of mechanical order for the fertile unpredictability of life) as well as by the direct cult of violence for its own sake.

Thus, we see that in a death-oriented society, even though it may seem very dynamic and powerful, death becomes the end of life in the sense of its goal, and this is made at least symbolically evident by the fact that money, machines, bombs, etc., are all regarded as more important than living people. In such a society, though much may officially be said about human values, whenever there is in fact a choice between the living and the dead, between men and money, or men and power, or men and bombs, then the choice will always be for death, *for death is the end or the goal of life.*

Nevertheless, this idea of death as goal, fruit or fulfillment is not completely false or misleading, once the context of sin is understood and accepted. But now death as "end" must be seen in a totally different light—the light, not of sin and selfishness, but of love and grace.

All created life is limited. Living beings come into existence and begin at once to develop, for growth is one of the essential functions of life. In the beginning of its growth, the living being must continually receive from others. The human infant, totally helpless and dependent on its parents, shows this clearly enough. In this state of vulnerability and limitation, the human heart already faces the problem of death, and it is here that infantile man, whose very nature it is to regard himself as interminable, as one for whom others have to live and sacrifice themselves, forms his cunning idea of death. But man's ideas must grow as he grows. The infantile concept of survival at any cost is a kind of absolute. It must be outgrown. As man grows into other stages of human development, he realizes that there are ways in which *life affirms itself by consenting to end.* For example, the youth begins to discover that by bringing to an end some egoistic satisfaction in order to do something for another, he can discover a deeper level of reality and of life. The mature man realizes that his life affirms itself most not in acquiring things for himself, but in giving his time, his efforts, his strength, his intelligence and his love to others. Here a different kind of dialectic of life and death begins to appear. The living drive, the vital satisfaction, by "ending" its trend to self-satisfaction and redirecting itself to and for others, transcends itself. It "dies" insofar as the ego is concerned, for the self is deprived of immediate satisfactions which it could once claim without being contested. Now it renounces these things, in order to give to others. Hence life "dies" to itself in order to give itself away and thus affirms itself more maturely, more fruitfully and more completely. We live in order to die to ourselves and give everything to others. This concept of "dying" is in fact altogether different from the death-loving attitude we have sketched above, for in point of fact this is not death-loving or death-centered at all. The "dying" to self in order to give to others is nothing more nor less than a higher and more special affirmation of life. Such dying is the fruit of life, the evidence of mature and productive living. It is in fact the end or the goal of life.

But since contingent lives must end—they are not interminable, and there is nothing whatever in their constitution that justifies us in thinking that they are—it is important that the end of life itself should finally set the seal upon the giving and the sacrifice which has marked mature and productive living. Thus man physically and mentally declines, having given everything that he had to life, to other men, to his love, to his family, and to his world. He is spent or exhausted, not in the sense that he is merely burnt out and gutted by the accumulation of money and power, but because he has given himself totally in love. There is nothing left now for him to give. It is now that in a final act he surrenders his life itself. This is "the end of life" not in the sense of a termination but in the sense of a *culminating gift*, the last free perfect act of love which is at once surrender and acceptance: the surrender of his being into the hands of God who made it, and the acceptance of the death which in its details and circumstances is perhaps very significantly in continuity with all the acts and incidents of life—its good and its bad, its sins and its love, its conquests and its defeats. Man's last gift of himself in death is then the acceptance of what he has been and the resignation of all final judgment as to the meaning of his life, its worth, its point, its ultimate destiny. It is the final seal his freedom sets upon the love and the trust with which it has striven to live.

For a Christian, this sublimation of death by freedom

and love can only be the result of a free gift of God in which our personal death is united with the mystery of Christ's death on the Cross. The death of Christ is not simply the juridical payment of an incomprehensible ransom which somehow makes us acceptable at the gate of heaven. It has radically transformed the sinful death of man into a liberating and victorious death, a supreme act of faith and love, because it also transforms man's life by faith and love. The obedience of Christ transforms the death of man into an act of glad acceptance and of love which transcends death and carries him over into eternal life with the Risen Christ.

For Christian theology, death "in Christ" is not merely a matter of external forms but of interior grace, and this grace can be and is given to every man, Christian or not, whose death is in fact the last free culminating gift in a fruitful life oriented to ultimate truth in God (whether known or unknown, but at least implicitly loved and sought).

Without the Cross of Christ, His love, freedom and grace, death grinds down upon the last despairing spark of life and triumphs over it because the spark, still clinging to its own illusion of interminability, refuses to give itself back to that from which it came. Hence various religious illustrations of this defeat: for Hinduism and Buddhism the man who clings to interminability must in fact go on being born over and over again, since that is what he does in fact want. In the Christian tradition this "interminable" loveless and meaningless existence is called hell. (We must, of course, remember that the graphic descriptions of hell's torments are more or less literary and are not expected to be taken literally just as they stand. Sartre's idea of hell in *No Exit* is in fact much closer to Christian theology than are the lurid pictures of devils and pitchforks pitching sinners into the hottest flame.)

The life of heaven, eternal life in Christ, is not simply a life without end. It is not interminable joy—even joy, if *interminable,* would become dreadful. The suggestive word "interminable" contains a hint that something that would be better terminated cannot in fact be put to an end. It never ceases! It goes on forever. Who would want a joy that he could never get rid of? Eternal life, on the other hand, has nothing in it which would be better if it were ended. The very concept of an end is no longer relevant, for the goal is attained. There is then no more goal, there is no end. All is present and all is actual. All is *pure reality,* the total compact fulfillment of man in love and in vision, not measured out in infinitely extended time but grounded in the depths of the personal life of God and the inner dynamic of love: from the abyss of the Father, in the light of the Son, through the love of the Holy Spirit.

Death is the point at which life, by freely and totally giving itself, enters into this ground and this infinite act of love. Death is the point at which life can, if we so choose, become perfectly real, not because it "demands to be interminable" but because it can receive the gift of pure actuality in the love of God, in the Trinitarian life, the circumincession of Persons. Death is then the point at which life can attain its pure fulfillment. Death brings life to its goal. But the goal is not death—the goal is perfect life.

Thomas Merton

FREEDOM

Beyond every life-draining definition lies the surging, purifying hope, refusing to be precisely pinned down like butterfly wings, smashing every stricture with the knowledge that such attempts are nothing more than guards against the dawn.

The word is known. In the subterreanean kingdoms where the meek are confined until the will is read, under black Mississippi earth and skies, by Harlem's curbside streams, in Peruvian hills and under Angolan trees, stretched out beneath the roaring sounds of star-spangled liberty in Vietnamese tunnels a generation old, from every fissure in the crusted earth, the word expands. In the sewers of the invisible the word lives and becomes such vibrant flesh that the threat always hangs hard upon the keeper's heart: "They may not wait to hear the will. They may not wait."

Among the wretched, weary with patience and yet cultivating it like poisoned tips of spears, no definitions are known and none is desired. What else could it mean but coming up for air, grasping light, finding food and strength to follow stars, to snatch lightning from the sky when they command and not fall prey to other electric hands? To lose the stoop so necessary in the hole, to be able to sin without the fear of fire bombs accompanying their song. To look into the rushing waters and see beauty (often black) smiling back, to drink from streams unpoisoned by the master's hand, to serve that Master whom the soul detects and him alone. All these are clear, clear as the smokeless, fumeless air when crusts are broken and men appear.

Only those who trample on the sacred ground, who spend a lifetime seeking out a cause while sitting on their brothers' earthen door, only the drifting, causeless, programmed former masters of the earth discuss the nature of this light, dissect the ontology of joy, refine the meaning of air. Only they decide when others are ready to sing and seek to say what songs are best for all newcomers to the day. For such, the night is defined as dawn and a noose resembles the lightning.

But let them pass. The crust is breaking, the songs will not be denied. The gasps for air will soon be thunderous roars. The long hiding will be over, but the revelation is not clear. Let definitions end, let the wings wrench clear; let freedom begin for all who know it by an instinctive calling of their souls. Dreary masters, leave the earth without the craters of your rage and perhaps a new race will emerge from the centuries of hiding to possess the land, claiming inheritance even before the will is read. Perhaps freedom will mean soaring and painful fall but never the tunnels again, never the sewers again. This much is clear this far.

Now refuse to be tied by words and let hope defy all laws of steep descent. Freedom? Freedom is . . . flying. Freedom is flying toward home.

Vincent Harding

About the Contributors

Frans A. M. Alting von Geusau is professor of law of international organizations at the Catholic University of Tilburg, the Netherlands.

Sister Mary Immaculate Creek, C.S.C., teaches English at St. Mary's College in Notre Dame, Indiana. She is the editor of *The Master and the Cross* and *The Cry of Rachel.*

James W. Douglass is an assistant professor of religion at the University of Hawaii. He is the author of *The Non-Violent Cross.*

Dennis Gabor is professor of electrical engineering at the Imperial College of Science and Technology in London.

Michael Goldman is an assistant professor of English at Columbia University. He is the author of two volumes of poetry, *First Poems* and *At the Edge.*

Vincent Harding is chairman of the history and sociology departments at Spelman College in Atlanta.

Charles Hartshorne is a distinguished American philosopher. He is the author of, among many books, *The Logic of Perfection* and *Anselm's Discovery.*

Hans Koningsberger's most recent book, *A Report Along the Roads of the New Russia,* was published in 1968.

Matthew Lamb is a Trappist monk studying theology and science at the University of Munster.

Deirdre Levinson lives in Davis, California. Her novel *Five Years* was published in 1966 in England.

William Lynch is the former editor of *Thought,* the Fordham University quarterly. He is the author of *Christ and Apollo* and *The Integrating Mind.*

Thomas Merton, a Trappist monk, died in Thailand in December 1968 where he had gone to learn more of the ways of Eastern religion. *Seven Story Mountain,* his first book, was his autobiography. Among his other books are *The Waters of Siloe* and *Bread in the Wilderness.*

Father Peter Minard, O.S.B., is the prior of The Holy Mother of God Monastery in Oxford, N. C.

George W. Morgan is University Professor at Brown.

John Nef is the founder of the Institute for Human Understanding of the University of Chicago.

Michael Novak is the chairman of the humanities program at the State University of New York in Old Westbury. He is the author of *A Theology for Radical Politics.*

William Pfaff is a member of the Hudson Institute. His latest book, written with Edmund Stillman, is *Power and Impotence: The Futility of American Foreign Policy.* He contributes a regular column on politics to *Commonweal* magazine.

Brother David Rast, O.S.B., is a Benedictine monk at Mount Saviour Monastery in Elmira, New York. He is studying at the Zen Study Society.

Ad Reinhardt, a painter, died in 1968.

Freya Stark writes travel books and essays. Her most recent book is *The Zodiac Arch.*

Peter Steinfels is an associate editor of *Commonweal.*

William Strickland is the chairman of the Northern Students Movement.

About the Editor

Ned O'Gorman is the author of four books of poetry. The last was *The Harvesters' Vase.* He works at the Addie May Collins Library.